DESTINY
YOU AND GOD

Barry M. Wood

BARRY
WOOD
MINISTRIES

Destiny: You and God
© Copyright 2010 Barry M.Wood

All Rights Reserved. No part of this book may be reproduced in any manner without the express written consent of the author, except in cases of brief excerpts in critical reviews and articles. All inquiries should be addressed to Barry Wood at barry@barrywoodministries.org.

Printed in the United States of America

Library of Congress Cataloging-in-Publication Data
Wood, Barry M.
  Destiny: You and God / Barry M. Wood
  ISBN-13: 978098-31-47305
  ISBN-10: 09831-47302

1.Christian Living   2. Theology   I. Title

Preface

Why a book about Destiny? Better yet, why a book about *your* destiny from a biblical worldview? When I have shared the ideas in this book with friends I have had two responses. One is genuine interest—people are very curious because "destiny" has become such a buzz-word in the 21st century. These days every strata of society is talking about destiny; everyone except the Christian community. That is a cultural fact worth looking into. Eastern religions and New Age thought is full of teachings about destiny. We who are Christians appear to be left out of this discussion as though our belief system does not include a strong sense of destiny. This brings me to the second response. Most Christians have a sense that "destiny" is only for others but not in the "life on earth" package for them. The only destiny most Christians think about is their final "destiny-ation"—Heaven. There is a misconception that all faith in Christ has to offer is personal forgiveness of sins and then heaven when we die. This entire book is about disproving that false notion. We who are Christ-followers must see ourselves as destiny agents who are destined to bring in the Kingdom of God.

We Long to Belong

The 2009 Academy Awards "Picture of the Year" award went to *Slum Dog Millionaire*; a movie centered on destiny. The movie follows a poor boy growing up in poverty in the slums of Mumbai, India. Jamal Malik, the young boy, is the slum dog. Jamal is an eighteen year old mysteriously "fated" to be a contestant on the Indian version of *Who Wants to be a Millionaire?* TV show. As destiny would have it, every question asked of him corresponded to an earlier life experience that gave him the answer to each question on the show. Conclusion—He was destined to win! Something or

DESTINY: YOU AND GOD

Someone was at work in his life fulfilling his destiny. This very popular film is a mirror of the hopes and dreams of millions today. We yearn for meaning, value and purpose. In the midst of the chaos of our lives we want to believe our existence matters. At the end of the film when Jamal is reunited with his childhood sweetheart, Latika, he says to her, *"We were destined to be together."* Wow! What a story.

Most people who saw that film may not be aware of the Hindu worldview that is behind the story. Eastern mystics have long viewed our lives as controlled by some unseen, unknown force that determines our fate. What is even less known is that our Christian worldview is very much about our God and His destined purposes for us.

It is my observation that Christians don't speak of destiny because the English words "destiny" or "destined" have not been a part of the Christian's vocabulary. After all, the word destiny is a "Johnny come lately" to biblical vocabulary. Only recent English versions of the Bible use the word "destiny" to translate a few Hebrew or Greek ideas. Conversely, in recent years ideas of "being destined" have consumed modern thought, media, and literature. One must ask why this is so important to today's pop culture and society in general? There are strong reasons for the current obsession with destiny which need to be understood. So, stay with me while I show you how to find your God given destiny and thus find life to be the thrill ride we all seek! Who knows maybe you were destined to read this book. It is all about God and you fulfilling your specific destiny.

Table of Contents

Preface: 3

Foreword: No God, no Purpose, no Destiny 7
Living in a post modern world without meaning or majesty

1. **From Your Mother's Womb** 13
   There is a pre-determined destiny for every life—even yours!

2. **Fated is not Destined.** 19
   Your destiny is in God's hands but you must choose it.

3. **The Bible—God's Destiny story** 25
   There is only one Story told in the Bible and it speaks of the Destiny of the Sons of men

4. **Men of Covenant are Men of Destiny.** 33
   Because God has made promises to significant men, we can hope for our significance also.

5. **Destiny and Religion** 41
   If God can choose a nation and call it to Destiny, then he can also call and choose us.

6. **David's Son—Destined for the Throne** 49
   The big story of history is about a babe in a stable, destined to become King

7. **Destiny and Your Salvation** 59
   Being forgiven is God's grace to us, being destined is God's purpose for us.

8. **Your Personal Destiny and the "Kairos"** 67
   When God shows up, your life is forever marked for Destiny

9. **Seizing those Destiny Moments as Opportunities** 81
   Redeeming the time means seizing those destiny moments.

10. **Destiny and Pre-Destiny** 89
    What's the big deal about predestination if it isn't about my pre-destiny?

11. **What a Difference a Day Makes** 99
    Meet Simon of Cyrene, you can learn from him.

12. **Men of Vision Fulfill Destiny** 107
    Plan your work, work your plan, but include your God given destiny

13. **Your Destiny can be Your Legacy** 117
    Your legacy should not be an afterthought when you live life on purpose.

14. **Who you Are and Who you Really Are** 127
    Sons of God are destined for greatness

15. **Destiny Demands Defiance** 135
    A life worth living is a future worth fighting for

16. **The Risk of Reaching for Destiny** 143
    Believing all God has for you requires us to risk what only faith can see.

17. **Destiny and the Call of God** 153
    God's call is greater than all our regrets and failures.

18. **Your Destiny as God's Mosaic** 163
    I've really screwed up my life; I'm destined to fail—really?

19. **Destiny and the Terminal Generation** 167
    The King is coming; will we live to see the last act of the drama?

20. **Finding Significance thru Destiny fulfilled** 179
    Moving from survival to success, to Significance thru an envisioned destiny

21. **Destiny and the Kingdom of God** 185
    Heaven just got better than you ever imagined

22. **But I was Afraid** 195
    Investing your life in the things that really matter

Epilogue 199

Footnotes 200

FOREWORD

No God, No Purpose, No Destiny

Living in a post modern world without meaning or majesty

"Destiny" has become an obsession with an entire generation in this young 21st century. People everywhere are talking about "destiny." Just listen to Oprah Winfrey and her guests, they are aflame with this new age light that they believe guides their futures. Strangely, Christians are seldom involved or included in this discussion. It is as though we are not very informed about destiny or its implications.

Could this simply be because we were raised on a biblical worldview that has not included ideas of destiny as a part of our Christian vocabulary? Yet modern society is fascinated by the idea of destiny. One must ask why this is so important to today's pop culture and society in general.

The 20th century began with an immense Christian optimism. Western culture, which was for the most part Christian, had been spreading like wild fire throughout the 19th century. By 1900 expanding European empires were taking the Christian message along with them to Asia, Africa, India, China, Indonesia and South America. Some were so optimistic about the advance of this world wide missionary movement that the 20th Century was being called the Christian Century! Boy, did they ever get that wrong!

Judeo-Christian Worldview

Behind this advance in Western culture was a Biblical worldview that today is being called by secularists a Metanarrative. The metanarrative, (meaning a big story or big picture) philosophy is the biblical story that Creator God is behind all human history working out His grand plan for human beings. The biblical metanarrative says history is going somewhere and that somewhere is where God chooses it to go. The big story told in the Bible is of God's continued struggle against real evil. There is the Kingdom of God in conflict against the god of this world—Satan. There is much destiny and purpose in the biblical metanarrative. The Bible story tells us men are destined for God's purposes to fight this conflict with Him and for Him. This was the worldview of the 19th and early 20th century. This worldview drove men like Christopher Columbus, David Livingston, and many others to explore and evangelize their world. They and others like them believed all men were "destined" to become one people in Christ. They were metanarrative thinkers—one truth, one story, one true God.

Destiny and Post Modern Thought

The world has changed radically since then. The 1900's gave us two World Wars, the Holocaust, tribal genocide, the rise of Communism and militant Islam. Western intellectuals began to see any metanarrative worldview as the tool of oppression and the instrument of destroying human rights and human freedom. They saw any "big story" system as a means whereby the rich suppressed the poor or the powerful subjected the weak. Over time we have seen the rise of an alternative worldview, now called Post Modernism. Post modern thought which rose out of secular humanism has blamed these big picture ideologies for all of society's ills. Post Modernism is not easily defined, but in 1984 when asked to define Post Modernism, Jean Francois Lyotard said, *"simply defined post modernism is incredulity towards metanarrative."* [1] Post Modernists find the idea that there is only one Creator God who has planned out all human history to be an absurd idea. In rejecting God and his big picture plans for humanity, they have abandoned belief in absolutes, or any metanarrative philosophy that they see as restrictive, tribal, or prejudicial.

For example; Marxist intellectuals in the very early 20th century were convinced the Communist/socialist ideal was the metanarrative for all mankind. In only 70 years their ideal society collapsed. Those same atheistic intellectuals were left with nothing more to believe in than consumer capitalism. Instead of the state being their god; self and self interests became the gods of choice. This is why post modern worldviews see no over-arching system of truth to believe in; so man has become the center of his universe. What the individual believes is true—becomes his truth. The same rejection of "big picture" narratives has happened with the Judeo/Christian model. Misguided liberal thinkers have faulted the biblical metanarrative as too narrow, bigoted, prejudicial, and oppressive. They say there is no one truth, no one creator god, no absolute good or evil. There is also no one all encompassing purpose. As a result modern societies have all but rejected any philosophy, religion, or social system that seeks to explain life from a "big story" point of view. Today this post modern worldview is the prevailing dogma and worldview in all our major universities. Our destiny has been taken away from us—no god, no destiny, no one reason to live.

A Worldview with No Destiny

So, when one does not believe there is a big picture purpose to our lives, then any thoughts of destiny become ludicrous. At least you would think so; right? However, Post Modernists in their rejection of the metanarrative have left themselves adrift in a vast universe like a ship with no rudder or sail... in fact why have a rudder or sail if you don't know where you are going! Without a sense of being connected to God, the "Universe," or something bigger than the individual self, post modern cultures are without values worth living for or dying for. We are discovering that to deny the existence of God's big story does not mean it is not true. A vital piece of God's big story in the Bible is that He created us in His image, with a God shaped hole in the human spirit that only the metanarrative purpose can fill. In every heart there are questions like:

"Who am I"?
"Why am I here"?
"Is there a purpose for my life"?

The post modernist answer is "Live for yourself, fulfill yourself and don't bother your neighbor in the process"! Well, thousands have tried it and found this narcissistic philosophy wanting. This may explain why there is such a fascination with Destiny today. A true Post Modernist cannot believe in destiny because to do so implies a universal design or cosmic designer. Yet a culture that is raised on the belief that there is no absolute truth, no overall purpose to human life still longs for this purpose and seeks connection to the "big picture" they are told does not exist. This to me explains why we have such obsession with destiny. In nearly all New Age ideologies destiny plays a vital part. Even in cultures that are essentially agnostic or totally secular, you will find multitudes that believe in destiny. They say things like, "I was destined to be here, or I was destined to do that, or it was fate that I met that person." It is inconsistent, irrational thinking, contrary to their secular worldview, but it is there none the less. Ever wonder why?

Connected to the Universe

We are so like Jamal in *Slum Dog Millionaire*. We too want to feel destiny's hand upon us, moving us along like pawns on a chess board. We too want to believe we are destined to win! That film truly does mirror our hopes and dreams of a bright future. Destiny is in the heart of all of us.

A glaring example of societies longing for purpose and meaning was the phenomenal success of Rick Warren's book *The Purpose*

DESTINY: YOU AND GOD

Driven Life. The success of a book by an evangelical pastor on the subject of God's purpose (destiny) for your life; written from a biblical worldview smacks in the face of secular humanism. This bestselling book is reminding us that we humans want to believe our existence matters and that we can be designated players in God's big drama.

Destiny and God's Story

This is why a book about destiny from a biblical perspective is needed. Our world has raised a generation that "knows not Joseph." The last two generations do not know the biblical story and therefore do not know the very good news that God has a destiny laid out for them if only they will believe it and live it out. The Bible is essentially the story of Creator-God and His predestined purposes for humanity. The Bible was never meant to be read as a book of rules, laws and moral precepts. It is a book of destiny—even your destiny. It tells us the love story of God and His lost creation and His desire to redeem us back to himself. The Bible tells us that our lives are not an accident; it assures us that God made us, and has purposes for us that are bigger than we can imagine. There is a big picture, a cosmic drama being played out and you can be a player in this drama.

You in Christ assures your Destination (heaven),
but Christ in you assures your Destiny.
—W. Ian Thomas:
from *The Saving Life of Christ*

CHAPTER ONE

From Your Mother's Womb

There is a pre-determined destiny for every life—even yours!

On May 14th, 1948, President Harry Truman, over much political opposition from his White House staff and Secretary of State George Marshall, voted in favor of support for a Jewish State in Palestine.

The released White House bulletin said, "*The government has been informed that a Jewish State has been proclaimed in Palestine... The United States recognizes the provisional government as de facto authority of the new State of Israel.*"[1]

Weeks later when Chief Rabbi of Israel, Isaac Halevi Herzog, visited the White House, he told Truman, "*God put you in your mother's womb so that you would be the instrument to bring about the rebirth of Israel after two thousand years.*" Another witness to the scene, Truman's administrative assistant David Niles, reported the President's reaction to Herzog, "*I thought he was over doing things,*" remembered Niles, "*but when I looked over at the President; tears were running down his cheeks.*"[2]

Truman and Esther

I have always been intrigued by Rabbi Herzog's words, "*you were put in your mother's womb so that...*" It is the "so that" phrase that points us to Destiny. The Rabbi believed in a God of Purpose who plans our birth, our lives, and our future. This idea that we are formed by God from the womb is a very real biblical truth.

Those of us who know the scriptures remember the story of Esther, a beautiful Jewish girl who became a Queen. She was an orphan raised by her cousin Mordecai, an official in the service of the Xerxes, king of Persia. Through a strange and inexplicable set of circumstances, Esther is among a group of young virgins chosen to be presented to King Xerxes. From this group Xerxes would choose a Queen. Remarkably he chooses the orphan girl Esther to become his Queen of the great Persian Empire. Later when Xerxes is about to put his name to a law which would exterminate all the Jews in Persia, Mordecai tells her that she must use her influence with Xerxes to spare her people.

> *"For if you remain silent at this time, relief and deliverance for the Jews will arise from another place, but you and your father's family will perish. And who knows but that you have come to royal position for such a time as this."*[3]

Put "on the spot" by her adopted father Mordacai, Esther makes a Destiny shaping decision. She will not be silent before the King. At supreme peril to her life she will plead for the Jews before her husband Xerxes. By His sovereign grace, God uses this beautiful and courageous woman to save the Jewish people from an ancient genocide.

King Xerxes executes Haman who plotted the Jews destruction and honors the request of his Queen. Today, the Jewish holiday Purim celebrates this deliverance. Esther is a child of destiny empowered and led by God. He has her at the right place at the right time to make the right decision. She is not a robot without a will or emotions. She can and must decide to risk her life to do what God has called her to do. Her faith and obedience are the deciding factor. Do you see the connection between Harry Truman and this ancient Queen? Esther and Truman were put in their mother's wombs *"for such a time as this."* Both of them followed their heart and fulfilled their destiny.

An Apostle to the Gentiles

Saul of Tarsus was a young and highly skilled rabbi. He lived during a crucial period in human history. Jesus, whom his followers called the Christ (messiah), has come on the scene while Saul studies in rabbinical school in Jerusalem. Jesus, arrested by the Jewish religious establishment, is beaten, and turned over to the Romans who crucify him. Soon rumors are everywhere that Jesus has been raised from the dead and is appearing to His followers. Saul, a devoted Jew, is outraged. He begins to persecute and even arrest these "Christ-followers." As an ambassador from the Jewish council of Elders (the Sanhedrin) he leaves Jerusalem to arrest those "Christ" heretics in the city of Damascus.

On the way, he has a dramatic vision when Christ manifests himself to Saul. Saul is blinded by the brilliance of the vision. Jesus calls Saul to become a Christ-follower. A few days later Saul receives the message that Christ has chosen him to be His instrument to take the Gospel to the non-Jewish world. Saul learns his destiny is to tell the gentiles about Jesus Christ. Years later Paul becomes so convinced that he was destined for apostleship to the Greek world, that he will say, *"But when it pleased God, who separated me from my mother's womb, and called [me] by His grace, to reveal His Son in me, that I might preach Him among the heathen."* [4] There it is again, chosen for Destiny from the womb.

This phrase "from the womb" is a continued theme in the Bible. Men of faith like Samson, David, Job, Jeremiah and others all see their destiny as planned by God "from the womb." This does not mean that God didn't think about their destiny until they were conceived in the womb, but it certainly means God has plans for us before we were born. *"Before I formed you in your mother's womb I knew you, before you were born I set you apart, I appointed you as a prophet to the nations."* (Jeremiah 1:5) Yes, that unborn fetus has God's name on it and God's future already planned for it.

This, *from the womb,* theology also tells us that you and I are not accidents of history, or even accidents of sexual union. God has His "designs" on us before we were even conceived.

From the Womb

A recent Super Bowl commercial produced by *Focus on the Family;* featured collegiate football star Tim Tebow and his mom. The commercial has a "from the womb" theme; Tim Tebow's mother was advised by her doctor to abort her pregnancy. Pam and Bob Tebow were missionaries in the Philippine Islands when Bob Tebow prayed for a son who would grow up to become a preacher. Bob even named the baby Timothy before Pam was actually pregnant. While pregnant, Pam became ill with a severe stomach amoeba causing dysentery and other complications. The physician feared for her life and for the life of her unborn child. After much prayer and soul searching the Tebows rejected the idea of abortion and trusted God to give them a healthy son. They dedicated the unborn child to God. After months of a very difficult pregnancy, God answered their prayer and a healthy baby boy was born to these fine missionary parents. That baby grew to become their dynamic son Tim Tebow, the first sophomore to win the Heisman Trophy. His is a "from the womb" story. The width and scope of Tim's destiny remains to be seen. God has given him a platform as a professional football player to fulfill his destiny.

What about you? Do you have any sense that God has known you from your mother's womb? That is an important question; because if you believe it then all heaven is on your side. But to reject the idea that you are fearfully and wonderfully made leaves you with little sense of being, purpose, or destiny. I personally choose to believe I am one of those chosen ones. Believing that there is a Creator God who loves me and has purposes for me gives eternal meaning and focus to my life. Knowing where I came from helps me find where I'm going.

The central and certain message of this book is that Father/God formed you in your mother's womb and "His form" in you is in the shape of destiny. In the pages that follow we will explore the issues that change, shape, or advance that Destiny. We have been given free will to choose or reject our destiny, and those faith choices are ours to make. When we walk humbly with God and seek to fulfill His purposes in the power of His Spirit, our lives make sense and make good on His choice of us.

DESTINY POINTERS

1. Knowing that God has known you from eternity past and purposed you from your mother's womb to be His child, what difference does it make to you?
2. In your life there are your plans and His plans. Are they the same, or are your plans fighting against your destiny?
3. Does it help you to know God has known you from the womb? In what ways does that affect you and your decisions in life?

CHAPTER TWO

Fated is not Destined

Your destiny is in God's hands but you must choose it.

The idea of destiny or fate to some is a pagan idea dating back to Greek mythology that has no place in a Christian worldview. At first this could seem true, but on closer examination we will see that God's dealings with mankind are ALL about our destiny as a race; and about His purposes for us as individuals.

Bible Language and Destiny

It may seem strange to talk about destiny from a biblical perspective since the English versions of the Bible tell the story without using our more modern word "destiny." As mentioned earlier, "Destiny" as a word choice is only now appearing in some of our newer Bible translations. This does not mean that the biblical metanarrative is not concerned with our future, our destiny, or our purpose in life. In fact, the entire story of God and His adventure-love affair with human kind is about where history is going—our destiny and destination.

The older vocabulary tells the story of God's will for us, or it speaks of God's purpose for men and even God's "call" on a man's life. All these are destiny themes in the story, each expressed differently. So, as we look carefully at the Bible's narrative, we see God taking the initiative to engage men in order to fulfill

His purposes in the earth. As He does so, men's lives are forever altered and their God given destinies are revealed. Those who walk in faith filled obedience to God's purposes discover their destiny and life becomes a thrill ride indeed!

Fate is not Destiny

The God Story of the Bible is that God created humans in His image for the purpose of having a relationship with them. The entire Genesis story is about God's destiny for mankind, how that destiny was lost through mankind's rebellion, and how a redeemer God began a plan to redeem and restore mankind to our original destiny.

It may be helpful to distinguish between "fate" and destiny. Ancient Greeks indeed spoke of fate as an irresistible force that determined one's future. The Greeks even personified their deities as "the Fates." This idea of fate as an impersonal force is not what we mean when we speak of your destiny. Destiny is not the French "que sera sera"—what will be will be." Being fated to do something is not an idea found in the Bible. Destiny has destination in it. Destination has purpose in it. To have purpose behind something requires a Mind and a Sovereign Being behind it. This is the central message of the Bible. God is the Master designer of the Universe. He created it and has purposes for it.

Destiny is Mystic Truth

If two people sit down to chat at a Starbucks, as millions do every day, the conversation can often turn mysterious. Recently I overheard my wife Gail telling a friend of a "destiny moment" in her life. While in Tanzania Africa on a medical mission, Gail and other Americans were in a remote Sukuma village doing HIV-Aids education and medical clinics. While standing near a dusty road, talking to an African man, a young Sukuma boy rode by on his bicycle. The youth's face was full of anger as he shouted at them as he rode by. Shortly after that, the lad rode by them a second time. Gail had not seen the youth, but an American man standing nearby sees the angry teen and tells Gail to talk to him. What happens next

DESTINY: YOU AND GOD

could be called mysterious by some, for it changed several lives forever. Thru an interpreter, Gail begins to talk to the youth. She tells him why the "wazungu" (white people) are here in his village. She tells him that God loves him and wants a relationship with him. The boy, named Juma, tells Gail he is an orphan whose parents died of Aids and he is alone with no future. That "chance" encounter with my wife changed Juma's life. Today he is our adopted son in school in Kenya, finishing his schooling and learning English to advance his education. Now you tell me—was that meeting of Juma and Gail a fluke of chance; or was some divine hand at work orchestrating it all. It feels like Juma was destined to meet a good lady who would love him and help him. To many of us it feels 'supernatural' doesn't it? The Bible says it this way, "*A man's heart plans his way, but the Lord directs his steps.*"[1]

Every day, ordinary people like you and I have these strange encounters that just seem beyond chance, reason or coincidence. They are not logical and even appear almost magical. How you view these "destiny moments" is the central theme of this book. Your worldview will determine how you will interpret these "destiny moments."

How you View your World

There is a worldview that is quite popular today that says we can know all facts and truth without belief in God or His existence. They say that all we need to know can be known through our human senses and reason. Those who live their lives by these presuppositions cannot accept the idea of destiny because it presupposes a cosmic plan or purpose. This worldview is commonly called secular humanism. I prefer to call it atheistic humanism. It is atheistic because it leaves no room for truth that cannot be known through human reason. To these folks if it isn't reasonable it isn't real. Out of this mindset has come post modernism that totally denies the concept of a big story that allows for destiny and purpose.

Secular humanism has left us without meaning, morals, message or majesty! They have removed the mystic and mysterious.

Leave a Little Room for the Supernatural

Another popular worldview says our knowledge of truth is only partly independent from God. What can be known through science and reason is true, but there is some truth that can only be known by divine revelation. Though viewed with some skepticism, this revelational truth is added to rational truth. There are multitudes of "Theists"(those who say they believe in God's existence) in the world today, but they are much more rational than spiritual. Their temptation is to minimize the revelation or to subject it to rational criticism.

Graeme Goldsworthy writes:

> "The theistic humanist is likely to see God as being subject to the same laws of the universe as we are. Thus we are able to draw up rules by which we decide what is reasonable. It is inconceivable that God could say something to us that is contradictory to reason. Human reason will therefore sit in judgment on the Bible to determine what aspects of it can be accepted as truth from God."[2]

This can help explain why some who believe in God fail to see and live out the destiny moments God has brought into their lives. God is working in and through human history every day but only those who look for destiny find it; others are too practical to see it. The Divine gets dumbed down to coincidence.

A Worldview open to Destiny

Those who see destiny are metanarrative people. Their worldview is that God created everything that exists—material and spiritual. He created mankind in His own image with the capacity to know Him from what He has created. Also, He created human kind as spirit beings capable of knowing beyond what is created, we can also know that which is disclosed to us by revelation.

The Christian theist also knows that man's knowledge is limited by sin. The fall of man in the garden is more than poetic language, it tells us facts about ourselves that we need to know. We are selfish, self-centered creatures who have turned away from our destiny and need to be forgiven and restored. This worldview, upon which this book is based, tells us that God's Word, the Bible, is God's story of how He intends to restore us to His original purpose for human kind. This restored life will lead us to destiny living. It can move us beyond our rebellion into destination living. We were meant to be much more than we are, and those who believe God's story can find themselves living out their part in the play.

DESTINY POINTERS:

1. Have you ever examined your worldview? Is it important to see your life from a Biblical worldview? If so, what kind of differences does it make in your life and the lives of those around you?
2. Does your worldview allow for the Supernatural to come into your rational world?
3. It does open doors to eternity if we are open to those "destiny moments" God brings our way. Do you begin a day looking for them?

CHAPTER THREE

The Bible—God's Destiny Story

There is only one Story told in the Bible and it speaks of the Destiny of the Sons of men

Adam in the Garden

So let the story of our human destiny begin. The destiny story has its origins in the first pages of the Bible, Genesis chapter one. We are told there was a beginning to the Universe; it came into being by a speaking Creator-God who spoke the worlds into existence out of nothing. Then out of His loving Father's heart He created man *"in His own image."* The narrative leaves no doubt that God had a destiny in mind for mankind. We were created for relationship with our Creator and man was given purpose for living. The story describes Adam and Eve, the first of a new race, placed in a beautiful garden where they *"walked with God in the cool of the evening."* They were fulfilling their destiny by living in fellowship communion with their Father-God. This by the way is what every man and woman was made for. Your very purpose for being on this earth is to know God and enjoy him forever. The very fact that so many of us feel lost in life, existing but not conquering, speaks to our need to be restored to fellowship with God. How we do that comes later in the story.

DESTINY: YOU AND GOD

Genesis then unfolds the story of man's position, privilege, and purpose. Created in God's image, we are spirit, soul, and body with potential and promise.

The story tells us:

Man is to be Ruler over all creatures upon the earth. Our destiny as a race is to have dominion. Our Father God is a Gardner-God who gave us the keys to the garden gate to keep it and enjoy its harvest. Genesis describes our dominion over the earth and it's creatures as our God given destiny.[1] Adam was told by God to name the birds, the land creatures and the sea creatures. It is worth noting, that you cannot rule over a creature you cannot name. To name it is to know it, understand it and have rule over it. We modern urbanized people of the 21st century can no longer name the animals—meaning we have lost touch with the earth and have become more the ruled than those who rule. To lose dominion is to lose destiny.

The Masai People

Much of my time the last few years has been spent in East Africa. Within the borders of Kenya and Tanzania live the Masai tribesmen. What a fascinating people group they are. For centuries they have lived within their natural environment. They live off the land and in harmony with the land. The Masai have "dominion", they can name the animals. By this I mean they know each and every bug, tree, plant, bird and animal intimately. The lion has lived side by side with the Masai people for a thousand years. The lion is not king of the Masai's jungle. He is fierce but the Masai is fiercer. He is deadly, but the Masai is even more deadly. The Masai Moron (warrior) respects the lion but he is not afraid of the Lion. In fact for generations the Masai warrior's initiation into manhood is to go out as a youth and kill the lion with nothing but his spear. This proves to the tribe that he has dominion—he has become a man.

The Masai youth cannot accomplish this courageous feat without first learning to "name" the lion and to thrive among the wild beasts. He knows them by name and by nature. He has

DESTINY: YOU AND GOD

grown up in a culture that teaches him how to survive. It is his destiny to have dominion over the wild beasts.

Every year as part of our mission efforts in Africa we take mission volunteers to an African game park for a photographic safari. It is great fun being in the Land-Rover stopped beside a pride of lions watching them feed on a kill. It is even more fun to watch the tourists who are looking at the lions. You can easily tell who has dominion and who does not. Some of our volunteers are so fearful they will not even look at the wild beasts—the lions, buffalo or cheetahs. They fear what they do not understand; yet the driver of the Land-Rover, who is also a game expert, is just the opposite. He does not fear the animals. He respects them but has dominion over them—he can name them.

There is a spiritual principle to be learned here about who you are and your place in God's economy. You and I were created to rule and reign over nature as sons of God. Just as every animal has its God created place and purpose, so do we have ours. We humans are at the top of the food chain in more ways than we realize. We humans are God's custodians of planet earth, destined to rule it and rule it well under God's care.

Man is to fill the earth. Genesis 1:28 says it is our destiny as a race to reproduce, creating a race of men and women to become a people for God's glory. This command to fill the earth is not just to populate the earth. Someone has truthfully said, "That's one command we have obeyed very well! We have made more mouths than we can feed." Over population of earth and over-reaching its resources was not the destiny God had in mind for us. Our sin and rebellion has led us to this place in history where millions are starving every day. More on that later. God's original command was for mankind to establish a race destined to be God's image bearers, His sons and daughters. Before man's rebellion in the Garden, God saw a people whom He could love and bless in a perfect paradise He created for them.

Man is to subdue the earth. Genesis 1:28-30 also says it is our destiny to subdue earth's bountiful resources. They are God's

27

gift to us to use and enjoy...We are to be a good steward of them. The earth is the Lord's; He created it and sustains it. The earth is not ours to squander or abuse, but rather we are destined to be stewards of the Master's garden, keeping it fruitful, enlarging it and subduing it's wildness for mankind's good and God's glory. This we have not done very well and have failed God and failed our destiny.

So we see the Bible tells us that we humans are very important to God, created with His purposes in mind. Destiny is in the heart of every man and woman. There is a God likeness in us that constantly draws us to Him and His destiny for us." *We find no rest till we find our rest in Thee."*

Adam and the Fall

Obviously something has gone very wrong. Eden was paradise with God center stage in the drama. However there is a villain in most good stories, and the Bible story of creation has a true villain. There was paradise with man living out his destiny as God's image bearer, then comes paradise lost. We are told that there was a serpent in the garden that could both talk and tempt. Now how are we going to take this narrative seriously with a talking snake central to the plot? Let me remind you that throughout its pages the Bible is a story. It is the greatest story ever told and it is a true story. The story form does not detract or lessen the veracity of the events. Can a snake talk and tempt? No, but Satan a powerful fallen arch-angel can appear as a talking tempting snake!

Paradise Lost

Far too many people have lost themselves and their destiny by losing faith in God's Word as a true historical narrative. Don't make that mistake or the serpent will have deceived you as he did the first couple. This tragic story is a tragedy for mankind. Adam and Eve are cast out of the Garden for the sin of wanting to be more than they were. God had created them a little lower than the angels, crowned with glory and honor (Psalms 8:5). The tempter convinced them that if they ate the forbidden fruit they would become as God himself. Ironically, there are plenty of revisionist stories telling us we are the same as God, or that we are destined to become gods or some such foolishness. The talking, tempting serpent is still at it!

So, let's go back to the story. The reason mankind is in such a mess and cannot seem to find its way out is vividly told in Genesis. Cast out of Eden the first couple begins the journey of fulfilling their destiny without God. They discover that destiny is all about their lost relationship with God. There is no human destiny apart from Him, only judgment and death. Man's rejection from the Garden was not a loss of paradise as much as it is their loss of presence—God's presence. A new presence has replaced God's fellowship; evil enters the story as Adam and Eve discover the cold reality of evil in their hearts and lives. Sadly they have learned the hard way that fulfilled destiny is very much tied to obedience. Just as God instituted natural laws of nature like gravity, He also established spiritual laws as well. The one Adam and Eve broke themselves upon was *"the soul that sins, it will die."* Destined to live under God's blessing, mankind now lives under the curse of death. Spiritual and physical death replace God's blessed destiny. Perhaps here we can define Destiny from a biblical perspective as "God's preferred future for His children." We can plan our own future but it will not be destiny; it will only be tragic and certainly not glorious.

The Genesis story is of paramount importance to our understanding of what reality is and what is mirage. Humans are caught up in a cosmic spiritual struggle between God and evil personified in Satan. This is not Reality TV—this is our reality! Every day we meet a fallen world, while the Garden Gate to God's presence and love is locked to us. We are cut off by our sin and rebellion from God's sovereign right to rule our lives. I hope you are getting this completely. Your God given destiny and preferred future is vitally connected to this Genesis story. Adam's "fall" from God's grace is your fall too. Just as Adam was God's son, we too are Adam's sons (and daughters). Just as God was in

DESTINY: YOU AND GOD

Adam, Adam is in us. His fallen nature is in every man. We have a spiritual DNA to rebel against God's right to rule our lives. This rebellion is destiny lost. Our purpose is summed up in this truth; we were made for God, to know Him and enjoy Him. Without Him we are lost to our true purpose for being.

Redemption and Restoration

Have you ever heard of Babel? You at least know of its meaning—to babble is to talk nonsense, or to fail to communicate. The word comes from a story in Genesis chapter 4, where we are told men gathered to build a tall tower to reach the heavens. God stopped their efforts by confusing their "tongues." The results were the creation of clans, tribes, and nations of men. The question on my mind is why did God do this? The story shows men trying to reach up to a God they had lost. The sons of Adam know only the stories passed down from generation to generation; stories of Eden and the glory of the days in the Garden. The Babel Tower to me symbolizes our human efforts to restore destiny. We are looking for a God and purpose we have lost; it is only a faint memory in our souls, only an echo of God's voice remembered long ago in the cool of the evening.

This could generally be said of all man-made religion. Religion arises out of the human need to feel connected to the big picture. Religion reflects the need in our hearts to restore lost destiny. We have lost God's smile upon us as favored sons and we want that smile back! Sadly all religion has done is create more babble! Do not be "babeled" (I think I just made up a word) into thinking that the biblical metanarrative is made of Babel bricks. It is not. God's story is not manmade—it is God's story, not mans'. It is a story about God's heart of love for the sons of Adam. John Eldridge has rightly said that the Bible is not a story by men about God; so much as it is God telling us about himself. God IS the story.[3]

How then can God restore what sin had destroyed? God's loving purpose is to bring mankind back to the Garden as paradise restored. The Bible calls it by another name—the Kingdom of God.

DESTINY: YOU AND GOD

The big story of the scriptures is that ever since the fall of mankind so long ago, God has been at work battling the forces of darkness to redeem, forgive, and restore us to our intended destiny. The story continues with God finding men and women of faith with whom He can covenant to restore mankind's lost destiny.

It seems that whenever God wants to re-direct the course of history He looks for a man to whom He can reveal himself. Here is where you and I come in. God is still calling out people of destiny through whom He can continue His redemptive purposes. He will continue to destine men & women until His Kingdom is fully established.

DESTINY POINTERS:

1. Is it important to believe in the Adam and Eve story in Genesis? If you do not believe it is true then how you can believe the other stories are true?
2. God's dealings with Adam and Eve tell us much about Who God is and who we are meant to be. What lessons can you learn from this Chapter that points you to destiny?
3. When we say that God's big story is about redemption and restoration, what do you think we mean by "restoration"?
4. How you see religion will reflect how you see God. Do you see religion as our human effort to gain God's favor? If so, is it a good thing to be religious? Can you fulfill destiny without being religious?

CHAPTER FOUR

Covenant Men are Men of Destiny

Because God has made promises to significant men, we can hope for our significance also.

If you read the Bible carefully you will "catch the plot" of the bigger story. God is up to something really big. He wants back what evil has taken away. A lost race and a lost planet must be returned to its Creator. His plan will be accomplished by men He can trust; men like Noah, Abraham, Isaac, Jacob and David. Then ultimately God will send His Messiah, the new David, Jesus of Nazareth to sit on David's throne forever.

Blood Covenants

God commits himself to these men by making covenant promises. The concept of covenant is not as meaningful to our modern cultures as it was in ancient times. A covenant promise was often a "blood covenant." It was a promise sealed in blood; like, "I swear to you by my life's blood." So we see God making covenant promises to certain individuals through history. These covenants are oaths God makes to himself and with men. He is promising that He has a destiny promise to keep with mankind. To fully understand our destiny we need to understand God's covenants with God's destiny agents. God will make covenant-promises with certain men that will bless all of humanity in ages to come.

God's Covenant with Noah—A Promise of Preservation.

Genesis six tells us God saw the wickedness of mankind, and it grieved Him that He had ever made mankind in His own likeness. The image was cracked! The sons of men had deserted their God and their destiny; sinking so low as to inter-marry with demonic creatures. God chooses Noah, for *"Noah found favor in the eyes of the Lord,"* and tells him to build a giant boat to save his family and select species of earth's creatures. God covenants with Noah to never again destroy the earth by flood.[1] However, the flood is also God's wrathful judgment on the failure of His old creation. It is the climax of paradise lost. God is starting over with Noah and his descendents; they will become the first of a new creation. Remarkably not much is really changed. Noah and his descendents are still sinners in need of grace and restoration; however, God shows himself more determined than ever to restore what was lost—He has a new destiny planned for those who trust Him.

God's Covenant with Abraham—A Promise of Blessing to all the Nations.
Genesis 12-22 and Galatians 3

This is the covenant upon which the entire biblical story hinges—God's promise and commitment to Abraham. Abram's destiny is forever altered when God renames him. Abram, meaning exalted father, is a wealthy herdsman living in ancient Iraq who hears the "call of God."

He is told by God to forsake his homeland and journey to a western land he had never seen. This was a true "destiny moment" for Abram and for all mankind. In faith Abram obeys and Abram's story becomes a "big story" that includes all of human kind. God's message to Abram is that his future will affect the future of all mankind. God wants to go into business with him and promises him a bright future.

Genesis 12:1-3 contains the terms and limits of God's covenant with Abraham:

DESTINY: YOU AND GOD

1. *"I will make your name great..."* Abram, meaning exalted father, becomes Abraham, Father of multitudes.
2. *"I will bless you..."* Abraham becomes a son of destiny as God's purposes flow through his life.
3. *"I will make of you a great nation"* From Abraham's loins will come a miracle baby boy, Isaac, who will father the nation of God's choice—Israel.
4. *"I will bless those that bless you and whoever curses you I will curse."* God's promise is that through Abraham's direct descendents (Israel) He will do His work of redemption and restoration. The Israelites are to become the people of destiny used of God to bring salvation to all humanity.
5. *"And all the peoples on earth will be blessed through you."* Here is the really big destiny story! God covenanted with Abraham that He has a planned destiny for all mankind. Be assured that what God promised to Abraham, He will perform. You and I can and should be recipients of that blessed destiny.

Isaac

The remainder of the "beginnings" story (Genesis) is about God miraculously keeping His promise to Abraham. The story continues with God giving Abraham and Sarah a miracle son when Abraham was 100 years old and Mama Sarah is 90. The boy, Isaac, is the child of promise through whom God will bless the world. Amazingly, God tests Abraham's faith by asking him to sacrifice the life of Isaac upon an altar to God. Although this command seemed totally unreasonable and contradictory; Abraham willingly obeys God by offering young Isaac as a sacrifice. In a destiny filled moment God intervenes and spares Isaac for His covenant's sake. God provides a Ram whose hair is caught in the nearby bushes. This miracle rescue becomes a symbol to future generations of how God provided a lamb, His Son Jesus, who would become the sacrifice for our sins. The story then shifts from Abraham to Isaac. Isaac and Rebecca have twin sons, Esau and Jacob. Even the birth of these twins is filled with destiny for all mankind. The story clearly shows the destiny of each twin, one to God's favor, the other destined to disfavor.

35

Jacob-Israel Son of Destiny

Jacob, the cheater, (his birth-name) becomes a type of God's re-creation. Jacob, son of Isaac, will become the father of twelve sons, who will become the 12 tribes of Israel. Jacob is transformed from a cheater/deceiver, into a man God can use. After years of a wasted life, he has an encounter with an Angel who gives him a new name and a new destiny. Jacob becomes "Israel" meaning prince of God. Israel's twelve sons and their descendents bless the world by providing a Messiah—God's anointed Savior who will die for our sins. This Savior is a direct descendent of Judah son of Israel. Judah's descendent is David, Israel's great king, warrior and poet. The promised Messiah is to be the "Son of David" destined to rule on David's throne.

One Story Many Plots

A word needs to be said here about the "big story" told in the Bible. Even though there are books in the Bible that are not narrative in nature, they are part of the story. For example, David and his son Solomon are very central to God's planned destiny for mankind. Yet we also see books and poetry written by them that seem unrelated to the ongoing "story." Books like Job, Ecclesiastics, Proverbs, Psalms, and others commonly known as "the writings" are still part and parcel to the greater narrative. They are not sub-plots or diversions. From reading these books we see the character, the struggles, and the God-man relationship that David, Solomon, Job, Esther and their kinsmen had with God. They are all vital to the story-line of the drama. They help show us our destiny and God's continued purposes for us as a Race.

God Destines Israel to Bless the World

The grand storyline of the Old Testament is God's fulfilling His promise to Abraham that through Abraham's "seed," He will bless the world. Israel as God's people has a destiny—it is their vocation to bring a redeemer/Savior into the world to sit on David's throne.

DESTINY: YOU AND GOD

Paraphrasing John 3:16, one writer says, *"for God so loved the world that he chose Israel."*[2] This choice of the twelve sons of Jacob (Israel) as his representatives on earth does not come without its problems. God's story becomes Israel's story also. Genesis tells us of Joseph, Jacob's favored and youngest son, who is sold into slavery by his jealous brothers. Joseph rises to prominence in the house of Pharaoh in Egypt and rescues his father, brothers and their families. The Israelites become a people in Egypt, though in bondage as slaves building Pharaoh's legacy. This however is not to be their prolonged destiny. God has bigger and better plans for these sweaty slaves working in Egypt's pyramids... They, like you and me are destined for glory.

Moses Prince of Egypt

God always looks for a man to use as He shapes human destiny. As Israel degenerates over 400 years into a nation of slaves in Egypt, God finds a hero to rescue them. That hero is Moses, whose name means "out of the water." God intervenes in the life of this Hebrew child, found by Pharaoh's daughter, hidden in a basket floating near the Nile. The boy grows up in the palace of the King to become a favored son of pharaoh, a Prince of Egypt. God sees potential in Moses that Moses does not see in himself. Through a strange chain of events Moses will murder an Egyptian and flee to the desert. His life is now linked forever to those Hebrew slaves. Seeking only to survive, Moses has his greatest "destiny moment," when God reveals himself to Moses in the form of a bush that burns, but is not consumed (Exodus three).

Israel's Great Escape

The accounts of Israel's escape from Egypt shout Destiny. God tells Moses to return to Egypt to rescue His people Israel. In Exodus 4:22, 23 God instructs Moses to say to Pharaoh, *"Thus says the Lord, Israel is my son, my first born. So I say to you, 'let my son go. Behold, I will kill your son, your first born"* When Pharaoh scoffs at God's command, God tells Moses of His plan to kill all the first born of Egypt. Only the homes whose doorposts have the

37

blood of a lamb smeared upon them will be spared. Those houses without the blood will experience the death of their first born. The Israelites do as God directs and are spared as the Angel of death passes thru the communities of Egypt. In the night, the Israelite slaves pack up and leave Egypt. Did you notice that God calls Israel His first born Son? This first "Passover" marks the sons of Jacob as God's son forever.

Israel God's Son

For God to intervene and rescue a nation of slaves is to mark them for Destiny. They are not just any people or nation—they are God's first born son. God tells Moses to tell Pharaoh *"Thus says the Lord, 'Israel is my son, my first-born."... "Let My son go, that he may serve Me."* (Exodus 4:22, 23) This means God has plans for His son Israel that take precedence over Pharaoh's plans. Israel's story is therefore God's story for humanity. God did not choose the Jews because they were better, smarter, or more righteous than other nations. They are chosen because they were destined by a Sovereign God who makes covenant promises. However because they are sons of the covenant (with Abraham, Isaac, and Jacob) God is faithful to them even when they are not faithful to Him. Israel is God's son destined to bring God's only begotten Son into the world. (John 3:14-16) They are a Messianic people.

Israel's True Vocation

When we think of the Jews in terms of God's calling; that is to bless the nations by bringing David's Son, Jesus the Messiah into the world; we can say they fulfilled their destiny. Yet, when we look at their history since their rejection of God's Messiah, we are led to believe Israel as a nation becomes the supreme example of failed destiny. Jesus himself predicted His nation's dismal future when He looked down from the Mount of Olives and said, *"O Jerusalem, Jerusalem, who kills the prophets and stones those who are sent to her! How often I wanted to gather your children together, the way a hen gathers her chicks under her wings, and you were unwilling. Behold, your house is being left to you desolate."*[3]

There can be no doubt that even though the first followers of Jesus were Israelites who became the early Christian Church; they and the apostolic leaders of the early church felt the judgment and condemnation of the Jews. They were persecuted by their own Israelite neighbors and rabbis. Soon, the apostles realize that Israel has failed its destiny to take the Gospel to the nations, so they turn to the Gentiles (non Jews) and the gentile church would extend Abraham's blessing to all the nations.

Israel as a Failed Destiny

We must not do as Israel did. Israel fixated on the Law of Moses, rather than on the Covenant message to Noah, Abraham, Isaac, Jacob, and David. Israel began to think they were chosen of God because they had the Law, while other nations did not. In so doing, they missed their greatest destiny moment. That moment was when God walked among them in the person of Jesus of Nazareth. Their time with Messiah was not only missed, it was profoundly rejected. God's purpose to bless the nations thru Israel passed them by. They have never recovered that destiny. There is a lesson here for all of us. We must always keep our eyes open to God's purposes in Christ. He is the message, the meaning, and the majesty of our being. Our destiny is found only in Him and serving Him.

What then is God's plan for Israel since they failed to embrace Jesus as their Savior? There are many of us today as Christian theologians who puzzle over the modern nation of Israel. Some think God is finished with them. Others, like me, can see God's judgment on the nation Israel for rejecting their destiny, but also hold on to the hope that there is still a restored future for a remnant of the Jews. We believe God's Covenant with Israel still holds, and that God has a future destiny for Israel. The Zionist movement that returned European Jews to Palestine and their ancient tribal lands in 1948 is seen by many of us as prophetic and an indicator of God's "last days" destiny for a Jewish remnant; who will return to faith in Christ as their king.[4] This is our hope and prayer.

A New Covenant Being Fulfilled

God will not fail to keep His covenant to bless the nations. Even though Israel as God's son has failed to keep the old covenant, God sent His true Son of David, Jesus, to establish a new covenant. Both Jeremiah and the writer of Hebrews see in Christ and His church a new and greater covenant promise.[5] The Church is to be God's new people, the bride of Christ, to carry the message to the nations. Jesus will commission His disciples to spread the good news that redemption and restoration are in progress. Our destiny depends on their faithfulness and His to bring it to pass. Future generations will be blessed by the message of hope and possible destiny fulfilled.

DESTINY POINTERS:

1. The Bible was never meant to be a rule book for moral behavior, or a set of principles to live by. Do you read the Bible and clearly see its bigger story? Do you often get caught up in its do's and don'ts?
2. The nation Israel was chosen by God as His people with a purpose and a promise. That purpose was to bring Messiah and salvation to the nations. Do you think they have failed that covenant? If so, what is their role in the Drama today?
3. When we say that the Church has become God's covenant people in this Age, does that impact you in any meaningful way?
4. Do you see destiny in your being in covenant with God through faith in Christ?

Chapter Five

Destiny and Religion

If God can choose a nation and call it to Destiny, then he can also choose and call us.

The curse of mankind is the distorted story told by religion. God's story and religion's story are vastly different. Religion's story is man-made, and originates out of a need in the human heart to find the Father-God we have lost. Heaven only knows the damage done to mankind by its religions. Man-made religion is demonic not divine. However it is worthwhile to explore the origins of religion in order to better understand ourselves and our need to fulfill destiny.

Freud and the Father

In the last century the father of psychoanalysis, Sigmund Freud, sought to reveal the source of man's need for religion. Freud said that we humans invented God and that all religion is the result of mankind needing to feel "safe" in a violent universe that seeks to do us harm.

Freud's idea, birthed in an evolution mentality, was that as we humans evolved, we created God in our own image. That's right, we created God! Out of our fears we evolved "religion" in order to feel that *"somebody out there likes me."* Freud would say that primitive religions produced primitive ideas of God, but that as man evolved (always upward) his ideas of God became more sophisticated until we smart humans began to see and worship God as our loving heavenly Father! Freudian thought says *"later religion is greater religion!"* Well, I don't think Sigmund Freud thought any religion was great! He did think that the idea of God as Father came from man's fearful heart, not God revealing Himself. Mr. Freud got it wrong. In fact he got it backwards. Let me explain.

Invention or Intuition

Where did this wonderful concept of God as our father originate? Maybe there is another and more life inspiring explanation. Could it possibly be that the biblical narrative is the truth? Yes, the Bible tells us God our Father created us in His own image because as a Father He desires relationship with His children. This Genesis story and the biblical narrative have a central theme running through it. God our Father wants a family—it began with Adam and Eve. Because of their rebellion, they were cast out of the garden and lost relationship with their Father/Creator. The biblical story tells us that humans have always known who we are and longed to know who God really is. This explains why wherever you find evidence of man's existence; you will also find evidence of his attempts at worship.

Mankind is essentially spiritual; God made us that way. This impulse to know God and restore relationship with Him is the result of an "orphan spirit" in the human heart. This is why I say Freud and his humanistic followers got it backwards. Modern man still longs for God as did primitive man. The God impulse is not external or psychological or an invention of man; it is internal. God made us for himself. When we are away from the Father, our orphan spirit cries out for restored relationship. You and your Heavenly Father together in relationship is your Destiny. In a sense we can say that all religion is our search for lost Destiny.

Religion and the Orphan Spirit

My good friend and Bible teacher Dudley Hall says, *"All orphan born religion features an unapproachable God and an approachable righteousness."* What a profound observation. Think about it—all religions feature first and foremost an unapproachable god. Regardless of the name you put on the religion, the god it presents is not your Father! He, She, or It is an unapproachable deity. We orphans feel separated from this deity, unworthy of his/her love, and in need of making great sacrifice to even get him to think about forgiving us of our sins, failures and brokenness. Read the Old Testament carefully and try to find God presented as a merciful, loving Heavenly Father. Good luck with that! The Old Testament does tell us that God is our Father, but it only does so in muted voice and in isolated revelations. Judaism itself knows of the one true God, but it only has a distant glimpse of Jehovah God as our father:

> Psalms 68:5 *"A father of the fatherless and a judge for the widows—is God in His holy habitation"*
>
> Psalms 89:26 *"Thou art my Father, My God, and the Rock of my salvation."*
>
> Deuteronomy 1:31 *"and in the wilderness where you saw how the Lord your God carried you, just as a man carries his son..."*
>
> Deuteronomy 32:8 *"You neglected the Rock who begot you, and forgot the God who gave you birth."*
>
> Isaiah 9:6 *"For unto us a child is born, unto us a son is given, and his name shall be called wonder counselor, mighty God, everlasting Father, prince of peace..."*
>
> Malachi 2:10 *"Do we not have one father. Has not one God created us?"*

It is worthy of note that throughout the Old Testament story you "feel" the fatherhood of God, but it is seldom directly stated. Until you get to the psalmists, God is often referred to as the "God of our Fathers." Then we read only a few sentences telling us God is like a father, but never does an inspired writer dare to believe that his God is *"our Father who art in heaven"*.

Describing Solomon, God says through the prophet Nathan,

"I will be a father to him and he will be a son to me" (2nd Samuel 7:14)

Speaking of God as creator Isaiah says:

"Thou art our Father, We are the clay, and Thou our potter; and all of us are the work of Thy hand"

Jeremiah looking into the future hopes the day will come when Israel will repent and see God as her heavenly father; *"You shall call Me, My Father"*. (Jeremiah 3:19)

These isolated passages are glossy glimpses into some wishful future when we orphans could know God as our father. It will take a Messiah come from the Father's house to our house to tell us that!

Judaism and the Orphan Mentality

These veiled references in the Hebrew Scriptures help explain why Judaism, the world's first great orphan religion, could not fully embrace the marvelous idea that Jehovah is also our Father. The Hebrew prophets see the twelve tribes of Israel collectively as Jehovah's son, *"You, Israel are my son, my chosen people."* Throughout their history God will call Israel His chosen Son, but only a few men like King David seem to be able to personalize this truth. It is a big step of faith to believe that God is my own heavenly Father who truly loves me!

In fact, the two great offenses that got Jesus of Nazareth in trouble with the leaders of Judaism was His perceived abuse of their Sabbath laws and His repeated claims that God was His Father. They never forgave Him for that! John 5:18 records their reaction, *"for this cause therefore the Jews were seeking all the more to kill Him, because He not only was breaking the Sabbath, but also was calling God His own Father, making Himself equal with God."* Jesus knew something wonderful about God His Father that the rabbis of His day could not comprehend. We will see more of Jesus teaching about His Father in another chapter.

DESTINY: YOU AND GOD

Allah and the Koran

Nearly seven hundred years later the Koran is written and viewed by millions as the inspired Word of God. Yet this God of the Koran, Allah, is not your heavenly father. I challenge you to find one reference in the Koran that describes Allah as the Father/Creator that the New Testament reveals Him to be. Islam is a prime example of another orphan religion. It offers the human race an unapproachable god and an approachable righteousness. Allah is great, Allah is one, says the Koran, but he is not your heavenly father. In fact Sura 4:117 declares *"Allah has no sons."* It makes sense that if Allah has no sons; then he certainly is not a father! Only Jesus the Son of God who was sent by the Father can reveal the Father. When read in this context the words of Christ take on a deeper meaning; *"no one comes to the Father, but through me."*

Fatherless Religion

Man-made religion will not portray God as Father. Religion, birthed from an orphan spirit, will long for destiny, meaning and a relationship with God but fail to get there. Dudley Hall rightly says, *"All religion is either seeking the Father or trying to define life without the Father."* This is vital to our understanding of who we are and why we are here. Destiny is connected to progeny.

The Bible tells us we were created by God with a capacity for relationship with Him. You and I, as god-like beings, were made for a Father-man relationship. Everything in your being is longing for and looking for this relationship with Father God.

Yet, our orphan spirit, which the Bible calls our sin nature, forbids us the capacity to believe we are not orphans on a treadmill of performance. This explains why orphan based religion not only touts an unapproachable God (how could God ever know the truth about me and still love me?), but religion always offers us an approachable righteousness.

When you and I have an orphan spirit or mentality we approach a relationship with God in a spirit of shame, unworthiness and guilt. We feel like outsiders looking in. We want to be in God's family, but feel we are not good enough. So, we create a religion that allows

45

us to be good enough. We create our own attainable set of rules; or we mistakenly think we can keep God's Big Ten commands. All religion does this. Man creates an approachable righteous standard he can achieve (or he thinks he can.) Why do we do this?

Performance

There are at least two reasons. First, we cannot believe that Creator God is also a loving Father. Jesus came into the world against the backdrop of the world's greatest fatherless religion—Judaism. When He taught that God was His Father and wanted to be their father, Jewish leaders plotted to kill Him. Second, we can't grasp that we are loved enough by Father/God that all we have to do to be accepted into His family is repent and believe the good news of His grace. Unable to believe this, we strive to be good enough. We hope to get to heaven (whatever we think that is) by pulling ourselves up by our own bootstraps. As orphans in a vast universe of endless humanity, we live our lives by comparison and performance. We long to belong and hope to find meaning and destiny. In order to survive futility we imagine that we can approach deity. Ignoring the words of scripture that *"there is none righteous, no not one;"* we continue to lower the standard. In our foolishness we think God grades on the curve! Well, He doesn't! Paul writes to the church in Ephesus, *"For by Grace you are saved through faith, and that not of yourselves, it is the gift of God; not as a result of works that no one should boast."* [1]

Hollywood Religion

James Cameron, Hollywood producer, behaves like an orphan looking for destiny. He and so many others in Hollywood are in love with their own version of Pantheism. Movies like *Avatar*, *The Lion King*, *Aliens*, *Terminator* and others preach a "pantheistic gospel". In these films, we are gods; made of the same "stuff" as the universe. This cinema theology tells us we are divine even as all of Nature is divine. Our salvation is to get in harmony with Mother Nature. You don't have to do anything except live in harmony with the planet and love and peace will come your way.

In this pantheist oneness there is no transcendent Creator God existing beyond nature and ruling over it. Oh no, the universe itself is divine and you are a part of the divine essence of all things.

That, my friends, is what we call an *"approachable righteousness."* It is man-made, convenient, and offers a sense of purpose. What is tragically wrong about it is that it has no Father. In this Hollywood pantheism there is no loving Creator God who wants to fulfill destiny in His children. It is an orphan religion trying to find meaning, love and purpose in a chaotic world. Apart from our Heavenly Father's initiative in sending His Son Jesus, we are destined to be homeless and fatherless in this vast Universe.

However, the message Christ brings us is that God wants us in His family. Through His sacrifice on the cross we can be restored, adopted and received as favored sons and daughters.

DESTINY POINTERS:

1. We have said that man-made religion is demon inspired not divine. How is it possible to tell the difference?
2. Do you fully understand what we mean by saying religion offers us an unapproachable God and an approachable righteousness? Why is this false and counterproductive to fulfilling your destiny?
3. In what ways do you approach God and relationship with Him as an orphan?
4. True destiny begins for us when we believe God is our Father through His Son Jesus Christ. Do you see God as your Father, or is He something other than that to you?

CHAPTER SIX

David's Son—Destined for the Throne

The big story of history is about a babe in a stable, destined to become King.

The Bible is a destiny book; it is the greatest resource we have concerning our destiny. Because the Bible is a book about God's redeeming purposes for mankind, it is a book fundamentally about God's Redeemer—Jesus. When we see God's destiny for mankind fulfilled in His Son, we can also see how our own destiny is connected to Him. So let me examine with you how Jesus is THE man of destiny.

The Promised Messiah

Destiny for Jesus begins before He is born. The Jewish prophets from Moses to Malachi had repeatedly foretold the coming of a Messiah whose destiny was to fulfill God's promise to Abraham to bless the nations. This coming Messiah is to be a descendent of David, born of a virgin in Bethlehem; He is destined to be both a King over a great Kingdom and a suffering redeemer at the same time. Isaiah writing in 700 BC, prophesied that the Anointed One would preach salvation to the poor, perform miracles, be rejected, despised, and tortured unto death. David in Psalms 22 and Psalms 69 foretells Messiah's torturous death by crucifixion hundreds of years before crucifixion even existed as a Roman means of execution. David again predicts in Psalms 16:10 that Messiah will be resurrected from the dead!

So, even a casual reading of the Old Testament reveals a "messianic theme" running throughout the Old Testament, all of which Jesus of Nazareth was destined to fulfill. Some 300 prophecies of Messiah's destiny are foretold and Jesus was destined by God to fulfill every one of them! Jesus will challenge those rabbis who questioned His identity by saying to them, *"you diligently study the Scriptures because you think that by them you possess eternal life. These are the Scriptures that testify about me."*[1]

There can be no doubt that Jesus believed He was the promised Savior. After His resurrection He is walking a roadway with some of His discouraged followers. These followers, thinking Jesus is dead, and not recognizing whom it was that is walking beside them say in despair, *"but we were hoping that it was He who was going to redeem Israel. Indeed, besides all this, it is the third day since these things happened."* (Luke 24:21) Notice the "past tense" which tells us their hope was gone, believing Jesus was dead.

It is then that Jesus identifies himself as the risen Lord and connects himself with Messiah's destiny. He says to these disheartened believers:

> *"O foolish men and slow of heart to believe in all that the prophets have spoken! Was it not necessary for the Messiah to suffer these things and to enter into His glory? And beginning with Moses and with all the prophets, He explained to them the things concerning Himself in all the Scriptures."*[2]

It is obvious Jesus firmly believed He was destined to be the promised Messiah and willingly embraced that role so we too might find our destiny in Him.

What's in a Name?

Even His name "Jesus" is a prophetic connection to His destiny. Gabriel an archangel appears to Mary, a virgin girl, with a pronouncement that changes her life and the lives of millions

DESTINY: YOU AND GOD

after her. She is to miraculously conceive a son and she is to name Him Jesus, meaning "Savior."[3] The angel forecasts the baby boy's destiny, for He is God's Redeemer to deliver us from our sins. Even His birthplace was destined centuries before His birth, when the prophet Micah predicts the Messiah will be a son of David born in David's village—Bethlehem. It took a taxation decree from King Caesar to make His parents go to Bethlehem from Nazareth for His birth. We can clearly see God fulfilling destiny day by day, step by step throughout His life.

Simeon's Prophetic Song

When the Christ child is eight days old his parents carry the babe to Jerusalem for the rite of circumcision. When they enter the Temple a stranger named Simeon approaches them and holds the baby boy high up over his head, proclaiming that this child is the long prophesized Savior/Messiah destined to be salvation both to the Jews and the entire world.[4] The entire narrative of the life of Jesus of Nazareth is written in the destiny zone.

John baptizes Jesus

As a young man Jesus comes to John the baptizer to be baptized by him. John sees Jesus in the crowd and declares, *"Behold the Lamb of God that takes away the sin of the world."* Jesus submits to John's baptism, but God has a greater baptism in mind; when in a destiny moment, the Heaven's part and the Spirit of God descends upon Jesus in the form of a dove. God's voice is heard by John and Jesus to say, *"This my beloved Son in whom I am very pleased."* This astounding announcement has immense destiny implications for all mankind.

Since the days of Malachi the prophet, the voice of God had been silent. God had not spoken to Israel in over three hundred years. The heavens had been silent, waiting for the coming of the long promised Messiah. Israel's rabbis had noted this divine silence and eagerly awaited the return of the "bath kol"—the voice of God. They knew that when the Messiah came, that the "bath kol" would return also. God's prophetic voice would be heard

51

again when a prophet like Elijah would announce the coming of the Messiah. John the baptizer was that voice of Elijah *"crying in the wilderness"* that Isaiah had promised. Both John and Jesus knew they were in a destiny moment when God's voice spoke to them. The Bath Kol had returned. They were the right men, in the right place, at the right time for destiny to be fulfilled. God's hand is upon them, as they walked destiny's path.

You and Jesus

This is a good place to affirm that all God was doing in the life of Jesus the Christ; He was doing for the good of mankind. All that is true of God fulfilling destiny in His Son Jesus, is connected to His destiny plans for you and me. The Apostle Paul will say it this way, *"But God demonstrated His love toward us in that while we were still sinners; Christ died for us."*[5]

Another way the Bible says it is that Jesus the Son of God came to bring *"many Sons to glory."*[6] What a fascinating phrase. Bringing *"many sons to glory"* speaks to our destiny. In fact, Paul declares it in very strong "predestination" language in Romans Eight when he states *"for whom he foreknew, He also predestined to become conformed to the image of His Son, that He might be the firstborn among many brethren."*[7] There you have it—you were on God's mind when He became flesh and blood and walked this earth. Jesus, man of destiny, lived and died for us and for our destiny connection to Him.

Jesus confronts the Enemy

Returning to the narrative of Jesus' life, He leaves the Jordan River baptism "filled with the Holy Spirit." He is walking in destiny's footsteps, simply obeying His Father/God. Led of the Holy Spirit Jesus goes into the desert where right from the start, His destiny is challenged by Satan. The Gospels tell the story dramatically as Christ is tempted to deny, detour, and destroy His destiny. Jesus meets Satan's challenge with firm resolve to do God's will, and resists the temptation to abandon God's plan for His life. As with so much in Christ's life, there is great teaching in this for His followers. Jesus was willing to fight for His destiny, and so must we. Satan wants to steal and destroy your God given destiny. You must resist him and fight to fulfill God's purpose for you. It will not come easily. You will need Christ's help and the indwelling power of His Spirit to accomplish your destiny.

Miracles as Destiny Markers

Jesus comes out of the wilderness temptation stronger than ever—His face set to do the Father's will. We see Him behaving the way the Son of God should behave—loving, healing, helping, and forgiving sinful lost people. He is a miracle worker the likes of which the world has never seen. Where sin, sadness, death and decay have prevailed; Jesus by His very presence or touch brings light to the darkness, turns sickness into health, and death into resurrection life. His miracles are called "signs." This means each miracle is a road map guiding us to a greater truth. The miracles are God's affirmation that He is with us and for us. Help is on the way—the Redeemer is among us. Each miracle performed is a destiny pointer to God's powerful intervention in the human drama. Just read the Gospels carefully and you will see Jesus the man of destiny bringing Heaven to earth in each mighty act. John's gospel chooses seven great miracles as proofs of Christ's mission and message. John climaxes his gospel with the raising of Lazarus from the grave. When Lazarus, bound up like a mummy, came hopping out of a dark cave—that was a destiny moment for the ages! It tells us that only Jesus has the power over life and death. This miracle is a destiny marker.

The Shadow of the Cross

Jesus was a man born for a great purpose. He was born to die. Years ago, Holman Hunt painted a lovely portrait of Jesus as a young carpenter, working in his father's shop. In the portrait, the young man is exhausted from a long days work and is yawning, stretching out his arms, you can see the wood shavings clinging to the hair on his arm. The painting has the evening sun coming through the small window. With arms outstretched, the young carpenter's shadow is in the shape of a cross. This was the artist's vision that the young carpenter had a greater destiny to fulfill. He was destined to die for our sins on a cruel cross.

Amazingly, the Messiah's sacrificial death for mankind's sins had been predicted long before by Israel's prophets. Isaiah graphically foretells the Messiah's death as God's chosen destiny for Him. Isaiah says,

> *"Surely he took up our infirmities and carried our sorrows, yet we considered him stricken by God, smitten by him, and afflicted. But he was pierced for our transgressions, he was crushed for our iniquities; the punishment that brought us peace was upon him, and by his wounds we are healed. We all like sheep have gone astray, each of us has turned to his own way; and the Lord has laid on him the iniquity of us all."*[8]

Fulfilling ancient prophecies, Jesus is destined for the Cross; it casts a shadow over His life. As He lives out His destiny as Savior/Redeemer, He continually comes in conflict with a lifeless, formalized Judaism of His day. The Pharisees who at first are amazed at Christ's teachings and obvious miracles, for their own selfish purposes begin to reject Him. They claim He gets His miracle-working power from the Devil, and they begin to openly oppose Him. It is not long into Christ's brief three year ministry that the religious Jewish authorities start plotting His death. As Isaiah prophesied, *"he is rejected & despised of men."*

Yet it does not deter Christ for one second. Matthew's gospel describes Jesus as *"setting His face towards Jerusalem."* The time and place reveal the sense of destiny in Christ's heart. He is in Caesarea Philippi—far to the north from Jerusalem, which is in the south. Jesus is as far geographically from His death as He will ever be. Maybe now is the time to run from His pre-destined, prophetically foretold death. Yet, He *"sets His face"* to go south to an impending death. Later He will say, *"No man takes my life from me, I freely give it."* He volunteers to face the cross as His God chosen destiny. He will die, that millions of Sons can be brought to glory (destiny).

DESTINY: YOU AND GOD

The Rest of the Story

I hope you are getting a bit excited about all this. You should be amazed that God planned all this for your benefit and future. It took God generations to bring it to pass. In bringing Jesus into the world, God was working out the greatest rescue operation in history. In one man's fulfilled destiny, Jesus the Christ, our destinies can be realized. He came for us. But we need to finish the story. Jesus unjustly dies a criminal's death by crucifixion. He is buried in the borrowed grave of a friend. However, this death is not God's final destiny plan for His Messiah. As Jesus himself predicted, God raises Him from the grave three days later. This resurrection miracle is the crescendo of the Jesus symphony. It is the greatest of the "sign" miracles that attest to Christ's glory as the Redeemer Savior. He has conquered our fiercest enemy—death, hell and the grave. The suffering savior of Isaiah is now the risen King of Kings, and Lord of Lords. He is the first of human kind to defeat death.

Our destiny is linked to Christ's victory over sin and death... He says to Martha before raising her brother Lazarus from the dead; *"I am the resurrection and the life. He that believes in me will live, even though he dies, and whoever lives and believes in me will never die."* [9] Later Jesus further connects His resurrection to those who believe in Him, when He declares, *"because I live, you shall live also."* [10] *Note* carefully that these are faith predictions on Jesus' part. He believes that God's destiny for Him and those who follow Him is resurrection life. To those of us who see Christ's resurrection as God's Destiny plan for us all, Easter can never be about Easter bunnies, spring time, or some other silly ideas about nature's birth or restoration. Easter is a glorious promise of destiny—life after death with our Living Lord and King.

Thy Kingdom Come

The Gospels tell us that after His resurrection from the grave, Christ repeatedly appears to His followers in His resurrected body. He is seen by groups of His disciples, and then individually appears to Peter and His brother James. 1st Corinthians tells us He also appeared to a crowd of 500 believers.[11] Jesus, man

DESTINY: YOU AND GOD

of destiny, isn't finished yet. The story continues to amaze and astound us. God the Father has a plan that includes restoring a Kingdom rule of God on earth. Jesus taught His followers to pray, *"Thy Kingdom come, Thy will be done on earth as it is in Heaven"*[12] His last appearance with His disciples was when He announced His return in the clouds with great glory to establish His kingdom.

So, it "ain't over till it's over"; the best is yet to come! My friend, you and I are destined for the Kingdom. Our Destiny is linked to Jesus fulfilling His destiny. It is the destiny and destination of all those who are believers in Christ to share in His coming Kingdom.

Day of Destiny

A few weeks after His resurrection, Jesus in the presence of His disciples, ascends into Heaven's clouds from atop the Mt. of Olives. Before leaving them, He promised to return on an appointed day. That day, the day of Christ's return, is one of those great days in history. The New Testament story repeatedly refers to Christ's return as "that day" or the "last day." It will be a day of destiny. I say that because that special day is in God's appointment book. It is on His calendar. His computer has it bookmarked. He knows when it is, and that day of Christ's return is predetermined in God's mind. Jesus told us that no man, preacher, prophet, or priest knows when that will be. Even the Angels do not know when that day will come. Jesus said that even He did not know—only God the Father.

When we say God knows the day, you can be assured it is destined to happen. King Jesus is coming for His people [the Church) and coming to end Satan's rule and to judge those who have served him. The practical implication of this is the fact that human history is not meaningless, cyclical nonsense. History is going somewhere, and that somewhere is Kingdom Come...Every single day that passes is bringing us closer to "That Day." Even more practically, we can believe that if human history is moving toward God's destination; we can also believe that our days are to be lived in light of that day. There is a day coming when the

DESTINY: YOU AND GOD

King of Glory will come to establish His kingdom. I strongly urge you to be preparing yourself to be ready to meet Him "in the air" when He arrives! Those who have crowned Him King in their hearts eagerly wait that day of destiny.

However, I am getting ahead of myself. The remainder of this book is given to exploring God's story of our Destiny in Christ. It is the theme of the Bible and the message of this book. Hopefully you will find it a fascinating adventure and maybe find your destiny along the way.

DESTINY POINTERS:

1. The very title, "Jesus Christ our Lord" has destiny in it. Can you see the progression? Jesus—references His death as our savior; Christ—references His resurrection; our Lord—references his Kingship over all things.
2. The Bible is totally about God's redeeming purpose to restore mankind. That means the theme of the Bible is Jesus. When you read it—Old and New Testaments, you should look for Jesus on every page. It will change how you read the Book.

CHAPTER SEVEN

Destiny and Salvation

Being forgiven is God's grace to us, being destined is God's purpose for us.

God loves a Lost World

Jesus said that His destiny was to *"seek and to save those who are lost."* He also knew the purpose of His coming into the world was to *"give His life a ransom for many."* The gospel of John says it beautifully, *"for God loved the world so much that He gave His only begotten Son, that whoever believes in Him, should not perish but have eternal life."* [1] There are several important destiny truths in this poetic verse. First, God sees us as perishing sinners in need of His mercy and forgiveness. The biblical worldview may not flatter us by calling us sinners, but the truth be told—sinner is what we are, and saving is what we need. Amazingly the scriptures tell us that God loves us in spite of our sin. He doesn't pick and chose whom He will love, but rather He loves all of us. The "world" is an inclusive word meaning the entire human race.

The Gift of His Son

The Father's desire to forgive us our sins cost Him dearly. The scriptures declare, *"But God demonstrates His own love toward us, in that while we were yet sinners, Christ died for us."*[2]

Sending Christ to die for us was not an afterthought with God. The Bible describes Christ as a *"lamb slain from the foundation of* *the world.*³ The Savior's gift was in God's destiny plan for those who would chose to receive the free gift of salvation in His Son. There is also meaning in the phrase *"only begotten"* Son. This term is used several times in scripture in reference to Jesus. It literally means "only borned one" or "one of a kind." Salvation is found only in Jesus, who is God's gift to us. Only His life and sacrificial death and resurrection can save us. Peter says it well in Acts 4 *"And there is salvation in no one else; for there is no other name under heaven that has been given among men, by which we must be saved."*⁴

Whoever believes in Him

This gift of forgiveness is received by putting our faith in Christ's sacrificial death on the Cross. His death is for all men and women but especially for those who chose to believe it is true. If you are a believer in Christ and have received this salvation gift, then you are saved! It's a done deal. However believing in Christ was a reflex action on your part. You did choose to believe in Him, but only after He first loved you. His divine love like the hound of Heaven came looking for you. You only responded to the Holy Spirit's urging and wooing. This divine initiative has destiny written all over it. Romans says it this way, *"and whom He predestined, these He also called; and whom He called, these He also justified; and whom He justified, these He also gloried."*⁵

That moment in time when God called you to repentance, and gave you the faith to believe, was your moment of destiny. At that very unique moment in history your destiny hung in the balance. You could choose to be saved or you could choose not to. There comes to those whom God calls a "destiny moment," when the Holy Spirit urges you to trust in Christ and Christ alone for your salvation. The old time evangelists used to say, "Being saved is a seeable, knowable, feelable, and datable experience." Those who reject God's gift of salvation have only one destiny. It is not really even a destiny so much as it is a destiny-ation. Their destination is to face God's wrath and judgment. *"He who believes in the Son has eternal life, but he who does not believe the Son shall not see life, but the wrath of God abides on him."*[6] For the saved there is eternal life, but for the lost only eternal death.

Salvation is also about Destiny

We evangelicals have probably missed the deeper meaning of salvation by placing so much emphasis on the initial salvation experience. "Being born again" has been our theme song. Having watched so many Billy Graham crusades, we have gotten the impression that all there is to being saved is to raise your hand, say the sinner's prayer and bingo you are saved and heaven bound. You are now "born again" and that's all there is to it. I mention this not to discredit Dr. Billy Graham—God has significantly used him as a man destined for this time in history. Billy Graham has always been my hero, so much so, that as a young man I followed in his footsteps as a young evangelist. I preached many a "crusade" in stadiums across America. I too asked people to come forward, pray with me, asking God to forgive their sins and be "saved." They did, and they were! However, in the context of the "big picture" your salvation and mine is important to Father-God in greater ways than we realize.

Beyond forgiveness and heaven as our final destination—there is our destiny. This destiny begins at our salvation experience when Christ the King comes to live His life in us. When He indwells us, He brings His kingdom rule with Him! This is where your destiny begins, as co-heirs with Christ. Salvation brings with it a new kind of living—the Bible calls it eternal life, or everlasting life. The conversion experience when we first believed is not however, intended by God to only be a "hit and run" experience that finishes the good work He has in store for us. It is only the beginning of a search quest of our destiny.

The mistake that is often made is that we think of eternal life exclusively in terms of living forever after we die. Many Christians associate eternal life as simply being in heaven sitting on a cloud with angels strumming a harp! Not so. Eternal life begins the moment you first believed. It starts the journey that leads to eternity in heaven. Eternal life as Jesus used the word is all about quality of life, not just quantity of life. God is interested in giving us the "life of the ages" which is the literal translation of "eternal." So, understand this, your fulfilled destiny depends on it. Salvation is mostly about your destiny. Our salvation is about life lived with a capital "L".

Life and Abundant Life

There are two words for "life" in the New Testament. There is the Greek "bios" meaning physical life, as in biology, the study of mammal life. Then there is the special Greek word used most often in the New Testament writings to describe eternal life: Zoë. This word "Zoë" describes the life that results from restored relationship with your Heavenly Father. Jesus said it this way, *"I am come into the world that you might have abundant life"* (Zoë). What Christ is offering is more than how long you live; He is offering us this Zoë kind of life. It is God's destiny gift from the Holy Spirit. It can abundantly restore us to destiny living in fellowship with our Father-God.

Adam as God's Son

To further expand on this eternal Zoë kind of life; let me return us to the beginning of God's story. It begins with Adam (the name simply means mankind) being created as a spiritual son of God. As a Father, God created us in His likeness in order to have a Father-son relationship with us. God is Spirit; therefore He is a Spirit/Father. Adam too is spirit, but clothed in flesh. The Genesis story of Adam and God in the Garden, as stated earlier, is about this abundant life (Zoë) that Adam had before his rebellion into sin. Adam's destiny was to be an obedient, loving son in fellowship with his Father. When Adam fell, he fell ten stories! It was a crash landing. We see Adam hiding behind a bush—ashamed of his nakedness. Where he had been in harmony and fellowship, walking with his Father in the evening's coolness; now he is hiding, isolated, separated from his Father and creator. Adam continues to live physically (bios life), but he is dead spiritually (Zoë life). He has lost life with meaning and destiny. All that is left for mankind is a bios kind of survival.

DESTINY: YOU AND GOD

Physical life is not about Destiny

The curse of sin that is pronounced upon Adam and Eve and their descendents is manifold in its results; but greatest of all is the loss of Destiny living. Created for fellowship with Father-God, Adam is cast out of Eden's Garden; he is cut off from "Zoë" which is abundant life. Adam has lost destiny. Man is the glove of God and God is the hand. As a glove is lifeless without a strong hand filling it, so mankind is lifeless and spiritually useless without the Zoë of God in him. This empty glove living is what Adam left us with. It is life lived without purpose, without destiny and obviously without God.

Since the fall, mankind has been forever looking for something more than "bios." We live our miserable lives often by the laws of tooth and fang. We have become like animals living only to satisfy our physical cravings. We have "devolved" into survivalists, rather than evolved into gods. Without relationship to God, we are lost to meaning and purpose. Yes, we need to be forgiven of our sins, but greater still we need to be saved and restored to our destiny as Sons of God.

Sons of Adam

This may help to explain for us our loss of destiny. For just as Adam was God's son, even so, we are all considered Adam's sons. Adam is created in God's image, but we as sons and daughters of fallen Adam are born in Adam's likeness. We have lost what Adam lost—the Zoë of God. This eternal life is both quantity of life—that is it lasts forever; and it is also quality and purpose of life. Better said, it is life lived in "abundance" as Jesus described it. He should know—He came from the Father, full of Zoë life, showing us what eternal life looks like. Jesus is God's Son living in perfect fellowship with His Father. Jesus is called the "second Adam" by the apostle Paul.[7] He accomplishes what the first man, Adam, failed to accomplish. Jesus lives out His destiny, which was to have been Adam's destiny, living his life in relationship with God his Father. In Adam we have destiny and eternal life lost; but in Christ the second Adam we have destiny and Zoë life restored.

Forgiveness and Eternal Life

So, we see that being "saved" is much more than simply being forgiven for what we have done wrong. Forgiveness pardons my past failures (sins) but it cannot make me a new creation. As a wise man once said, "Sin is an inside job" meaning my nature is to commit selfish acts—sins. I need a new nature. My heart and yours is like a sin factory that keeps producing more and more sins. Each day I need more and more forgiveness. This defeated, shame filled life is not our destiny. It is Adam's curse upon us. We need someone to close down the sin factory, and give us a new heart. This is why I'm telling you there is much more to being saved than just being forgiven and having a ticket to Heaven. Our destiny which was lost in Adam's fall can be restored in Christ Jesus our risen Lord. He has Zoë life in Him and He desires to share it with us.

Those who only think of salvation in terms of forgiveness will never comprehend the concept of being saved as being a part of God's greater purposes. Those who live out their God given destiny are those who see salvation in terms of the bigger picture. They are those who are allowing the Zoë life of God to be lived out in them and through them. In this sense, the abundant life Jesus offers his disciples can be seen as the life God intended Adam to live before his rebellion in the Garden. The abundant life becomes destiny living, fulfilling God's purpose for your life.

Christ Followers with little sense of Destiny.

There are so many serious Christian believers who are clueless as to their destiny. Life for many of them is about obeying the rules (like the Ten Commandments) or desperately trying to live the Christian life through their own efforts, strength or good works. Many Christians are so consumed with the bios life, they have little energy left for destiny. I would challenge any of you my readers to stop long enough to seek God, seriously asking Him to reveal destiny living to you. I am not speaking of just asking God for some grand plan for the rest of your life, but rather being open to His abundant life and purpose for just one day at a time. To be truly saved is to be a new creation in Christ and to be indwelt with the eternal life of Christ. He wants to fulfill His purposes in and through you. When He is allowed to manifest His love and grace through you, the result will be destiny fulfilled for that day or moment in time. Then and then only can this sentence in Ephesians begin to make sense to you in the light of Destiny fulfilled:

> *"For we are His workmanship, created in Christ Jesus for good works, which God prepared beforehand, that we should walk in them."*[8]

Did you notice the phrase, *"created and prepared beforehand?"* Friends that's about destiny living. It tells us that God has planned your day before you were born. Abundant living which fulfills destiny only comes to those who are willing to "walk in it," one day at a time. Can you believe that as God's forgiven child you are His workmanship? Can you also believe He is working out your salvation destiny according to His kingdom purpose each and every day? Try it, you'll like it!

DESTINY POINTERS:

1. How do you see "being saved"? Does it carry with it the strong idea of being destined to join the story of God's bigger purpose? Or, do you only see your salvation in Christ as being forgiven and going to Heaven when you die?
2. Being a Christ-follower means you have His Zoë life abiding in you. Are you experiencing the power of that extended nature of Christ living out His life through you? This is where destiny begins and is fulfilled.
3. Most people I ask have little or no sense of destiny. How can you as a Christ-follower begin to live in His Spirit and fulfill destiny?
4. God-given Destiny is only for those who are adopted into God's family through faith in Christ. What is your obligation to tell others of how they too can know Christ?

DESTINY: YOU AND GOD

5. How do you balance the acceptance of your salvation and destiny living with your efforts, strength and good works? What is your motivation? To just be "good" or live your life with a godly inspired purpose every moment of every day?

CHAPTER EIGHT

Your Personal Destiny and the "Kairos"

When God shows up, your life is forever marked for Destiny.

A few years ago, a pastor friend of mine invited me to lunch; he had something important to tell me. This pastor in his younger days had been with me on a mission to Kenya. We had coached a basketball team using basketball to share Christ's love with Kenyan high school kids. During lunch he tells me he wants to return to Kenya and needs me to use my many contacts to set up the mission. I was honored he included me, but I told him I had been there—done that. I was not interested in going back. He urged me to reconsider, even suggesting that he would lead the sports ministry and I could train some pastors in a conference while we were in Kenya. I respectfully declined. Not to be denied he suggested we talk again the next week, which we did with much the same result. It did not appeal to me to go 9,000 miles from home to teach a few pastors how to pastor! Much of my resistance was due to my decision to finally retire from active ministry.

A Destiny Moment

Shortly after those two meetings with my pastor friend, I was reading my Bible one morning, just enjoying God's fellowship. I had no real idea that God would speak a clear word to me that day. While reading in Psalms, I came to Psalms 71:18 which states: *"Even when I am old and gray, do not forsake me, O God, till I declare your power to the next generation."* (NIV) In that moment in time something supernatural happened to me that reshaped my destiny. I read those words, reread them, then I "heard" those words in my spirit. God spoke destiny into my life. It was one of those "destiny moments" when God showed me what I was to become and do during "retirement." I do hope you believe with me that none of us who are serious Christ -followers are ever meant to retire!

The Next Generation

How was I to show God's power to the next generation? What younger generation wants to learn anything from a senior citizen? I was a bit puzzled, but also excited. Over the sixty plus years of my life, most of it in ministry, I had much knowledge and wisdom stored up in this gray head of mine; but was anyone really interested in what I had to teach them—that was the question? Then, almost mystically, God began to show me who he had in mind as the next generation—Africans. God began to fill my thoughts with how I could mentor a generation of young African leaders. I knew that there was almost no written material on discipleship in Kiswahili—the national language of 13 East African countries. I became convinced that God wanted me to show His power to an entire generation of young African leaders. The way to do this was for me to write a leaders discipleship manual and give it to whomever wanted to read it.

Learn to Type Son

This was utter foolishness, because at age 60 I did not own a computer or know how to type! So I bought a PC, and a book called Microsoft for Dummies and looked for the page to tell me how to turn the thing on! Really—it's the truth. Six months later I had created a 175 page manual for African leaders. The pastor and I began to plan our Kenyan mission. We hosted a Key Man conference, inviting 100 young men from Uganda, Tanzania and

Kenya to attend our conference for a week of training. That was June of 2001. Since then over 5,000 men (and women also] have attended our Key Man leadership conferences in seven East African countries.

The Power of a Destiny Moment

Are you getting this—it all started when God interrupted my life! He entered my space and claimed it for himself. I was not looking for destiny but destiny came looking for me. Amazingly, this experience I had of a Destiny moment is very common throughout the biblical narrative. God has shown He has a habit of "intervening "when His eternal purposes intercept our time.

Chronos and Kairos

God is involved in linear time—human history. He is the God of our yesterdays, today, and all our tomorrows. (Hebrews 13:8) He is the Sovereign Lord of time. He numbers our days, meaning He sees a man's life in an instant, and sees our future as though it is today.

In the New Testament there are two very different ideas about time. In Acts 1:7 Jesus says to his followers, *"It is not for you to know times or epochs which the Father has fixed by His own authority."* In this sentence are two often repeated New Testament words.

Chronos—The first is the word most often translated "time or times." It is the Greek word "chronos". Our English word chronograph comes from this word. A chronograph is an instrument like a watch that measures time. Chronos always describes time as sequential, linear, and accumulative. When describing chronos we use such phrases as "killing time," "it's about time," or "time is money." Chronos is always about the ticking of the clock, or as we frequently say, "the passing of time."

Kairos—The second word translated as time is the Greek word "Kairos." It has a very different meaning. Kairos often means simply a season, an epoch, or a date in time. In 1st Thessalonians 5: 1 we read, *"Now as to the times and the seasons (epochs), brethren you have no need of anything to be written to you."* Here Paul is telling us

69

that there is Chronos and Kairos. It helps me to understand this by seeing time (chronos) as quantity of time; whereas Kairos (a date or season) is quality of time.

Kairos as a Destiny moment

However, Kairos can also mean a "Destiny moment" when God is doing something eternal in the midst of temporal. A Kairos moment is what God is doing during the chronos (time passing). Another way of saying it is, "the Kairos is the significance of the time." Kairos is God's purpose behind the chronos. For example we are told in scripture that Jesus was born "in the fullness of time." The word translated "time" here is Kairos—not chronos. Jesus came into the world at a Kairos moment in human history. God sent him here to intervene in the midst of our history. The birth of Christ was a huge destiny event for both God and humanity.

Biblical Examples

The Bible is full of divine punctuation marks when God in a destiny moment moves in history (the chronos) to fulfill destiny.

Abraham is visited by the Lord (three angelic men) who tell him that aged and barren Sarah will become pregnant with destiny's child, the boy Isaac. (Genesis 18) That was a Kairos moment, when God gave significance to Abraham's life.

Abraham is again the recipient of a Kairos moment when he willingly lays Isaac upon the altar and raises the knife to sacrifice his precious son, only to have an Angel cry out for him to not slay the boy Isaac. God then provides a ram whose horns are caught in the nearby bush. That was another destiny moment in the lives of Abraham and Isaac.

Samson, Israel's great warrior judge becomes a man of destiny. After miserably failing God and his people, mighty Samson is blinded and used like an oxen to grind meal for the Philistines. Feeling his shame and failure we see Samson ask God for one more opportunity to avenge himself and to glorify the God of Israel by destroying the Philistines and their pagan God Dagan. Samson's prayer is answered and in a Kairos moment Samson's

DESTINY: YOU AND GOD

supernatural strength is restored. Flexing his strong arms Samson collapses the columns that support Dagan's temple. In a moment of time (Chronos) Jehovah God added Samson to the role call of God's champions. It was another of those "destiny moments."

Rabbi Saul is on the road to Damascus to persecute the followers of Christ. He is a zealous Jew, ready to defend Judaism and defeat the new sect of the Nazarene. Then in a blazing Kairos moment his life is forever changed. The resurrected Jesus appears to Saul in a blaze of glory, so much so that Saul is blinded by the brilliance of the vision. That encounter with Christ on the road that day not only changed Saul's destiny, but the destiny of millions more as well.

So many more

The Bible is replete with story after story of these Divine encounters that turn the chronos the way God wants it to go. You cannot read the scriptures without seeing that Creator/God has a grand plan and He is determined to carry out His purpose. Also, these Kairos intrusions by God are not limited to only the biblical narrative. Histories pages are full of these Kairos moments that rearrange the landscape of human destiny. There are Kairos moments in every life—even yours. You may not recognize it, but God is ever seeking to engage us in His destiny purposes.

Martin Luther

Young Martin Luther was a wild, godless German guy when one day riding along on his horse, lightning struck so near him that he was thrown off the horse and came crashing to the ground. Luther was terrified, thinking the lightning was God's warning to him to repent of his sins. Martin was so convinced this lightning strike was a Kairos moment that he joined an Augustinian monastery to save his soul. There, after years of searching for peace, he finally came to the scriptures in Romans 1:17. Again, God showed Luther how to find peace in accepting Christ's free gift of salvation by simply believing it was true. Those destiny moments in Luther's life produced the Protestant Reformation in the Sixteenth century that changed history once again.

71

DESTINY: YOU AND GOD

Abe Lincoln

Abraham Lincoln was a man used of God to fulfill destiny. Many stories have been told of Lincoln's multiple failures and even severe questions as to Lincoln's faith. Was He a Christian or an infidel? Only eternity will answer that question, but this much I know—Lincoln's life has the mark of destiny upon it. When Lincoln was out of politics for all practical purposes, and practicing Law in Illinois, he had come to hate slavery and saw the harm it was doing to the Union. He returned to the political stage as a result of the 1854 Kansas-Nebraska Act. This Kansas-Nebraska Act had been written to form the territories of Kansas and Nebraska. It included language, designed by Stephen A. Douglas, which allowed the settlers to decide whether they would or would not accept slavery in their region. Lincoln saw this as a repeal of the 1820 Missouri Compromise which had outlawed slavery above the 36-30' parallel. He returned to politics to become a leading opponent of the Slave Power—that is the political power of the southern slave owners.

Behind Lincoln's becoming the Republican candidate for president in 1860 was his strong desire to stop the spread of slavery in the new territories. When elected president and in the midst of the civil war, Lincoln felt God's hand upon him to abolish slavery. He writes, *"I have been driven many times upon my knees by the overwhelming conviction that I had nowhere else to go. My own wisdom and that of all about me seemed insufficient for that day."* Abraham Lincoln is a prime example of a man who strongly sensed he was destined for his time and place in history. He lived out his destiny moment. God used this very strong man to abolish slavery in the United States. Proverbs 21:1 declares, *"The king's heart is like channels of water in the hand of the Lord; He turns it whenever He wishes."*

Mandela

Nelson Mandela is another icon of destiny. A few years ago I read Mandela's biography. It is a stirring book telling the story of a courageous and stubborn man. There is little evidence in Nelson Mandela's life to indicate he is a Christian in the traditional or evangelical sense. Yet when I look at this remarkable man's life, nearly thirty years of it spent in prison in South Africa, I cannot help but see again how *"the Lord turns the hearts of kings like channels of water."* Mandela's life-long passion to abolish Apartheid in his home land has the mark of God's purpose stamped all over it. So you see a man like Mandela, Lincoln, or even Pharaoh become men of destiny when they are used of our Sovereign God for His purposes.

The Kairos today

Much of my own personal growth as a Christian and a human being has come through my ability to see, feel, and respond to these Kairos visitations from God. When I respond to the Holy Spirit's nudging, destiny moments happen with clarity and power.

In 1969, while pastor of a church in Beverly Hills, California; I was reading the Los Angeles Times sports page. Jim Murray, the famous sports writer, had written an article about a Hall of Fame football star named Dixie Howell. Murray outlined in his essay the heroics of Alabama quarterback Dixie Howell in the 1935 Rose bowl game against Stanford. I was fascinated reading Murray's sports column, as he recalled the events in one of the most fabulous bowl games ever played. It seems Dixie Howell, Don Hudson, and Paul Bear Bryant all played on that University of Alabama team. [1] Then Jim Murray's column revealed that Dixie Howell, now in his fifties, was in the Hollywood Presbyterian hospital, diagnosed with cancer and waiting for surgery. That hospital is only ten minutes from where I sat reading the newspaper.

Although I had never heard of Dixie Howell, I knew of Bear Bryant and Don Hudson. In that moment the Spirit of God spoke to me saying, "I wonder if Dixie Howell has a pastor. Barry, you need to go see him in the hospital." I knew immediately what I must do. I got in my car and pointed it in the direction of the hospital.

Now, I tell you this story to confirm that when we are sensitive to God's voice, we can experience these incredible destiny moments. When we are alert to these Kairos moments, God can work his miracles in us and through us.

DESTINY: YOU AND GOD

A Kairos Moment

When I walked down the hallway to Dixie's room his lovely wife Peggy was outside the door. I stopped, introduced myself as a local pastor, wishing to see Dixie Howell. Peggy told me she was Mrs. Howell and broke into tears. She said, "I'm so glad you came, I have been praying for someone to talk to my husband." I asked her if Dixie was a Christian and she replied no, but that he is a really good man. What happened next can only be explained in terms of destiny. Dixie Howell the famous athlete was about to experience his finest moment. While talking to Dixie as he lay on the bed, I asked him if I could pray for him to be healed of his cancer. Dixie said he had lived his life without much time given to God or spiritual things. Then he said a noble thing, "I haven't given the coach (God) much credit, so it doesn't seem fair to ask for His help now." It was then that I said to this fine man, "Dixie, if Jesus will heal you and get you back on your feet, will you live for Him in the days that He gives you?" With strength in his voice Dixie said, "Yes, I will." I then prayed for his healing and Dixie Howell asked Christ to forgive his sins and become his savior.

The rest of the story is worthy of Paul Harvey. God gave Dixie nearly three significant years of health. I baptized him; he began to grow in his faith, and he and I became close friends. He and Peggy introduced me to some of the most famous people in Los Angeles, which opened many doors for me to witness to God's love. Dixie lived out his pledge to live as God's man. He played hard for "The Coach" until the day he died. When the cancer returned, I saw Dixie's faith and trust in the Lord. I was with him when He died. He had been in a coma-like state for awhile, but in a remarkable moment of consciousness, Dixie raised his hands from the bed, his eyes closed, and said one word, "Jesus." Then he left us to complete his destiny.

What a Funeral

Wait; there is more to this story. I was the preacher at Dixie Howell's funeral in Beverly Hills. The little 200 seat chapel was packed as great athletes of the Dixie Howell era came to pay their respects. Johnny Mack Brown, Glen Davis, Don Hudson, and many others attended. There was a Military Honor Guard and a delegation from Alabama Governor George Wallace in attendance to carry Dixie's body home to Alabama by private plane. In my eulogy, I spent very little time recounting Dixie's exploits in football, baseball, and coaching. I alluded to them, but hurried on to share the Dixie I had known the last two years. Knowing Dixie to be the humble man that he was, I told of Dixie's love for God, his faith in Christ, and how he went out like a champion serving His Coach. That funeral was a glorious testimony to the goodness of God.

Hartford Alabama

Dixie's destiny story isn't quite over yet. In all my association with Dixie, I knew he was from Alabama but I never knew where in Alabama. He was from the small town of Hartford. Strangely, without my knowing why or how, in about 1973 [two years after Dixie's death] I received an invitation from the Pastor's Association in Hartford Alabama. They wanted me to preach a county-wide evangelistic meeting. Now the strange thing is I did not know that Hartford was the home and burial place of Dixie Howell.

He's Buried Nearby

I arrived by private plane just in time to preach. A large crowd had gathered in the National Guard Armory building. As I began my message, I was eager to "connect" with this Alabama crowd. So, I thought to myself "how can I make a connection with these folks?" So, I began to tell them the story of my relationship with Alabama's favorite son—Dixie Howell. Now mind you, I did not know Dixie was from this very town! When I began to tell Dixie's story there was a stir, even a buzz in the crowd. I could not figure out why the crowd was so excited about this story.

After the message many people came up to me to tell me about their friend Dixie. It was then I discovered Dixie was a native of this very community. Indeed one pastor told me, "Dixie Howell is buried not 100 yards from here in the cemetery behind this Armory building. What a moving experience it was for me, when the next morning I stood looking down at my friend's grave. Looking back on it now, I can see that God was fulfilling destiny to bring me into Dixie's life and he into mine! I haven't seen the last of Dixie and Peggy. We will meet again—I'm sure of it.

The Louis Lapides Story

Louis Lapides is a highly successful Christian leader in Los Angeles. He is the former senior pastor of Beth Ariel Fellowship, an evangelical Church in Sherman Oaks, Calif. A Jewish Christian ministering to a secular culture, Louis has made a significant impact on the destiny of thousands. You might be surprised to hear how his destiny story began.[2]

Sunset Strip 1969-70

In the spring of 1969 I became pastor of the small but strategically located First Baptist church of Beverly Hills, California. This was the summer of the Charles Manson killings, hippies and the beginnings of what became known as "the Jesus movement." Runaway youth from all over the U.S. were congregating on Hollywood's Sunset Strip and street evangelist Arthur Blessitt was there sharing Christ's love as well as others.

I'm not certain of the date, either in 1969 or 70, Arthur Blessitt chained himself to a Cross & telephone pole outside the Whiskey A-Go-Go (a popular night club on Sunset Blvd.). Crowds began to gather each night to see Arthur Blessitt during his month long fast. Many believers were there praying with Arthur and witnessing to passers-by. One summer evening I was there on the street with Arthur and others, when a young Jewish guy comes walking up to see what was going on. I introduced myself to him. He said his name was Louis—Louis Lapides. That night I remember my first encounter with Louis; he was a skinny 20+ year old John Lennon look alike. He had curly black hair, wire rim glasses, was thin and a dead ringer for Lennon!

DESTINY: YOU AND GOD

"I don't own a Bible"

As I engaged in conversation with Louis, he revealed to me that he was a Jew, but not a "practicing Jew." I began to ask him what he knew about Jesus Christ and the Bible. Louis tells me he is not religious, but that he is a Jew and cannot even think about Christ. I challenged him to read his own Bible (the Old Testament) and see for himself that Jesus is the promised messiah and the fulfillment of 300 or more prophecies made by the Hebrew prophets. That's when a "destiny moment" occurred. Louis, seeking to put me off track said, "I don't have a Bible so how can I know what you are saying is true?" Standing nearby, listening to our conversation, was an anonymous Christian guy dressed in khaki's with concrete on his boots. Evidently he was a construction worker and had come straight from work to witness that evening on Sunset Blvd. This guy, whom I had never seen and have not seen since, had a new expensive leather bound Bible that he had just purchased. He took that Bible, opened it to the dedication page, and wrote something like this, "To Louis, may reading this book lead you to your messiah." Whether he included his name I cannot remember. I'm sure Louis Lapides knows; because Louis took that Bible and began to read it for himself, to see if Jesus is who he claims to be.

Save me Jesus

A few weeks later, I was preparing to preach on a Sunday morning when to my utter surprise, in walks Louis Lapides. I did not totally recognize him, but he did look familiar. After the services Louis comes up to me and I hear the most amazing story. Louis had gone out into the Mojave Desert and while on a LSD drug induced high was reading the Bible given to him by the nameless construction worker. He was reading from the book of Revelation. As he was spacing out on LSD, he had all these visions from Revelation in his head. He was terrified, thinking he was dying. In a destiny moment, while clinging to the rocks, he cried out, "Jesus save me!" And Jesus did save him—completely and absolutely! I baptized my hippie friend Louis Lapides, helped get him a scholarship to a Christian university, never dreaming this John Lennon look-a-like druggie would become the mighty man of God he was destined to be. All these events, these "Kairos moments" came together to bring Louis into the Kingdom. He was destined for greatness in God's purpose.

Your Destiny Moments

These multiple snapshots of God intervening in the lives of others are given to awaken in you my readers a passion for God's story to continue in you. You must not remain a spectator, God wants destiny to be fulfilled in your life day by day and moment by moment. You too were meant to be destiny's child.

First, the journey begins by faith in Christ. When He enters your heart, His purposes can begin to take place through His life within you. If you are not a serious Christ-follower, become one right this moment. Let destiny begin in you as you repent of your sins and receive Christ as savior and God as your Father.

Welcome the Kairos

Destiny minded believers live in expectation of those Kairos moments. They define, direct, and determine our destiny. They know that the joy of life is seeing the Kairos invade the chronos. The words of Proverbs become reality to them: *"The mind of man plans his way, but the Lord directs his steps."* (16:9) Serious Christ followers welcome the Kairos moments, for that is when God shows up to invite you into the Drama of the Kingdom. The Kairos moments are "Kingdom Come" prayers fulfilled in your daily life. You realize that you are simply the actor-God is the actual producer, author and director of YOUR play and YOUR life. It takes the pressure off you to extemporaneously "perform" and allows you to follow the lead God is quietly providing you. So, the remainder of this book is designed to help you fulfill your God given destiny. Although destiny is often mystical, we will seek to make it practical as well. Our Father God eagerly desires to "direct your steps." Hopefully we can together learn how best to respond to His call and direction for us.

DESTINY: YOU AND GOD
DESTINY POINTERS

1. So, you have learned about the chronos and the kairos. Each day that passes (the chronos) you have opportunities for God to invade your day and present the kairos moment of destiny. What would you have to change to make this a daily experience for you?
2. It will bless you to recall those kairos moments God invaded your life. It begins in salvation, the day you were born again. Recalling those kairos moments will create in you a hunger for more.
3. Do you think some people are sensitive and alert to the supernatural presence of God? How can you develop your own sensitivity to hear God's voice or see His intervention?
4. Every day there can be a God-event if you are open to His callings and His favor upon you. Look for the kairos and it will appear as surely as the Sun rises in the East.
5. Instead of trying to write, produce and direct your day why not try to live tomorrow as the actor—listening and following those divine nudges instead of getting frustrated when moments don't go as YOU planned?
6. Do you think it would be life changing for you if you began your day by asking God to direct your paths and declare himself to you?

CHAPTER NINE

Seizing Those Destiny Moments and Opportunity

Redeeming the time means seizing those destiny moments.

Seizing the Opportunity

As we have seen, God has many destiny moments He brings into the lives of His children. They happen millions of times a day all over the world. These "kairos" moments are the fertile ground for destiny to blossom. This idea of kairos, often translated from the Greek to mean a season or a "God event" can also mean an opportunity. Paul uses the word this way in Galatians when he says, *"While we have opportunity (kairos), let us do good to all men especially to those who are of the household of the faith."*[1]

Thus used, a kairos moment becomes our God offered opportunity to respond to destiny. The English word opportunity has Latin roots. It comes from an old source—"ob portis' which pictures a harbor with its changing tides. When the water is at high tide it is "ob portis" or opportune; so it is with our lives. Those God given moments are our opportunities to obey God and enter into His purpose; when missed; they become for us destiny missed and opportunity lost.

Macedonian Call

A clear example of a God offered opportunity is recorded in Acts 16. Paul the great Apostle was in Troas, Turkey when a nighttime vision came to him. We can assume it was while he was sleeping. In this dream Paul sees a man from Macedonia appealing to him to "come over" and help us. The "come over" part is the Aegean Sea. So Paul must cross an ocean to answer this call for help. Remarkably, Acts records Paul's response to this kairos opportunity saying, "...and when he had seen the vision, immediately we sought to go into Macedonia, concluding that God had called us to preach the gospel to them." I see several life lessons we can learn from this. The first is that Paul is so sensitive to the Holy Spirit that he can discern when a dream is just a dream or when it is a vision of a divine opportunity. Paul concluded that God was speaking to him through this vision.

How about you, are you that sensitive? Think about it, how many opportunities have you missed by not hearing God's voice because you were not listening carefully enough. The kairos came and you missed it. The dream was from your Father and you took a sleeping pill to escape it! When we miss enough of these divine appointments, we become hardened to the supernatural and begin to see them as intrusions on our comfort. It is then that our lives become dull, without destiny, meaning or fulfillment. Paul's simple act of obedience changed the course of human history. He was headed east toward Asia and God called him to turn west. He had to cross the sea to obey, but obey he did. That one singular act of seizing the opportunity took the gospel to Europe rather than to Asia.

Secondly, I see that Paul did not hesitate, but he *"immediately sought to go into Macedonia... and made a straight course for Samothrace* (on the coast of Europe).[2] I can just see Paul's excitement. He says to Silas, his traveling companion, "Go book us seats on the boat—we are going to Europe to tell them about Jesus!" The lesson here is that we must quickly obey lest the opportunity pass us by. When God brings us to the threshold of destiny's door—we must enter immediately. How many times have you had those "high tide, ob portis" moments when you should have acted and didn't; only to learn later that it was opportunity missed. God was at work and wanted you to participate but you let it pass you by.

I see a third lesson for us to apply here. Paul *"concluded that God had called us to preach the gospel to them."* Friend, you have to train yourself to do that. Those who are too rational will miss the revelational. God's callings are not always as obvious as a Macedonian man in a dream. Sometimes you might be eating lunch at a restaurant, busy talking up a deal with a client, when the waiter comes by your table and you casually say to him, "how are you doing?" You are only making "verbal noise" with no real intent to know how he is "really" doing. Then, the waiter says, "oh I'm okay," but his body language is telling you he is not okay. As he walks off, you try to pick up your business conversation with your client, but a voice is speaking to you down deep in your spirit. It is bringing that waiter's remark to your consciousness. God is asking you to seize the opportunity He just presented to you. You are feeling a strong urge to engage the waiter in further discussion, maybe even to minister grace to him in some God ordained way. Now what do you do? Obey, or rationalize. Reason would tell you that you are here on business and to ignore your silly emotions. This is not the time or place to get involved in a strangers life. Has anything like that happened to you? I promise you it has if God's Spirit dwells in you. He calls us daily to be salt and light in the lives of others. Salt penetrates and heals, while light dispels the darkness.

The Middle of the Night

You really do have to train yourself to live for and look forward to the kairos opportunities. Seizing those moments comes from intentionally seeking them. A few years ago I was hospitalized a few days to recover from major surgery (is there any other kind?) Before I received the "gas" to put me under I prayed a private prayer telling God I wanted to be a blessing to nurses, doctors, and all who attended me while in their care. The first night I was there I was given much pain medicine to help with the recovery and so I was out of it for the most part. The night nurse came into my room to check my vitals and although I only vaguely remember this, it seems that at 3:00AM I spoke to the nurse; telling her I am a preacher and asking if I could pray for her about anything. She began to tell me her very sad story. She had been retired, both she and her husband. Before they could enjoy their retirement time together, he came down with cancer. She had been at home for three years caring for her beloved husband. When he died, she had come back to nursing just to be active. They put her on the night shift as a starting job. I asked her if she was a Christian. She said yes but she was very angry at God for the sickness and death of her husband. Even in my drugged state of mind, she told me later the next night, that I took her hand as I lay in the bed and I prayed for her asking God to heal her pain and restore her joy so she could be used to love and care for others. She wept, and thanked me. I tell you this so you will know that I did not even remember this conversation! She told me of it the next night as she was making her rounds. Somehow God's Spirit in me was strong enough to seize the opportunity to love on this nurse even through my medicated condition. You really do have to train yourself to look for the kairos opportunities God sends your way and pray that it becomes your habit to find them.

Obstacles and Opportunities

Opportunities come in many shapes and sizes. Not all opportunities appear to be good or even seem to be opportunities on the surface. Some opportunities appear to be obstacles rather than God given opportunities. Often we have seen that what Satan meant for evil God meant for good. I was recently reading in Mark's gospel when I came across the story of Jesus using a storm to teach a lesson. It reminded me that some of the really big storms in my life have turned out to be God ordained opportunities.

Let Us go over to the Other Side

Mark's gospel tells a most remarkable story from the life of Christ that vividly illustrates his sense of destiny.[3] Jesus is in a boat on the lake in Galilee. He tells his disciples, *"let us go over to the other side."* So, a caravan of boats set sail for the other side of the lake. Tired from his ministry to the huge crowds that follow him, Jesus falls asleep in the boat. In the middle of their passage across the lake a fierce storm arises and all in the boats are terrified fearing they might perish. The frightened disciples awaken Jesus and cry out over the storm, *"Rabbi, do you not care if we die?"* Jesus then speaks to the storm and tells the wind and waves to "hush- be still;" and the lake became calm. The disciples are astounded! They say to one another, *"who is this man that even the wind and the sea obey Him."*

That was not a question they were asking but rather a declaration they are making.

Maybe I'm missing the point here but my mind fastens on the beginning of the story—before the storm. Jesus tells them to *"go over to the other side"* knowing full well (at least sensing in His spirit) that the storm was a possibility. Did he want to teach his followers that He is Lord of the storm? I think so. In your life and mine many storms come our way that God not only permits but He plans. He does so to advance His kingdom.

Keepers of the Mosque

Barry Wood Ministries has many African staff in several east African countries. Each year we gather the staff for an annual retreat. Recently one of our men, David Mukhaye from Kenya, told the staff a most interesting story. David and his assistant were somewhere in Kenya preparing to show the Jesus Film in a city center. Several thousand people were gathering for the outdoor film showing when storm clouds began to gather. Before the show began it was certain the rain was coming so David began to gather up his equipment to protect it. So quickly did the storm arrive that they had to hastily look for cover from the storm. The only building that seemed accessible was the Mosque. David and his assistant opened the Mosque door and began carrying equipment inside. In they came, two soaked evangelists, along with their generator, screen, sound system, DVD player and projector.

DESTINY: YOU AND GOD

Hearing the commotion, two Muslim men who worked at the mosque came walking over to them and asked, "What are you doing in here?" David told them they were about to show their film when the rain came so they ran inside to protect their film equipment. I don't think David told them what the film was about (Jesus); but the two Muslim guys welcomed them in. David held in his arms a large one foot by one foot Evangecube.[4] One of the Mosque custodians looked at the Evangecube and asked, "What is that you have in your hands?" David said something like, "I'm glad you asked." He then proceeded to use the Evangecube to tell the gospel story of Jesus to those two Muslim keepers of the mosque. When David finished the story, he asked them if they wanted to have their sins forgiven and receive Christ as Savior. Both of them said "yes!" That stormy afternoon, God stilled the storm in those two guys' hearts. They found salvation right there in the Mosque.

Now, in light of the story of Jesus and the storm, what do you see in David Mukhaye's experience? Did our Father God cause a rain storm to cancel a film showing in order to bring his two witnesses into that mosque for the purpose of introducing two keepers of that mosque to faith in Christ? Does God even control wind and rain to bring men and women into their destiny? What do you think? Think seriously about it. How many times has God used men, events, sickness, accidents, even nature itself to bring you to a place where you could finally see what those disciples saw. They exclaim, *"What kind of a man is this that even the wind and the waves obey his voice!"* Those kinds of moments are kairos opportunities when God steps into our lives and advances the Kingdom; fulfilling His destiny purposes. God will even orchestrate the storms in our behalf. If God is for us—who can be against us? All we have to do is trust Him in the midst of it.

Living on the Edge of Eternity

Ever wonder what eternity is going to be like? I'll talk about that in the last chapter of this book, but for now let me give you an insight. You and I do not have to die to go to heaven. Heaven can be your daily experience in the here and now, rather than in the sweet bye and bye! Those moments when God chooses to invite you into His drama are eternal glimpses of the glory to come. Every time the kairos enters your day you are living out destiny. You are on the very edge of eternity. When we obey those destiny callings we are extending and expanding the ministry of Jesus upon the earth. Those opportunities are your privilege to bring the Kingdom of God into someone's life. The more often you obey those callings, the more likely God will trust you with bigger and better opportunities to fulfill your destiny. One day at the Bema Seat your rewards will reflect the power and magnitude of that destiny you lived out. This is living at its finest. You were born for this. Paul said it well, *"Christ in you the hope of glory."*[5] *That* means the glorious life you were destined to live is fulfilled when Christ is allowed to manifest His life in and through you. He will call you to those marvelous opportunities to bless others, but He will never call you to do anything that He is not capable of doing through you. All he asks of us is to obey and leave the results up to him.

Therefore, I urge you to listen carefully, to look intently, and to avidly seek the kairos moments God brings your way. He desires to use you if you will only be alert and quick to respond.

DESTINY POINTERS:

1. Are you looking for the *"and immediately"* moment God brings your way? They will come to you in direct proportion to your "and immediately' obedience to it.
2. Understanding your God given opportunities as destiny defining moments will add excitement to your existence. You can move from existence to significance as you see God directing your steps.
3. Why do you suppose most people cannot see or take advantage of those kairos events God brings? Are you missing many of them yourself?
4. Ask yourself what you must do to be more available to God so He can fulfill destiny in and through you.

CHAPTER TEN

Destiny and Pre-Destiny

What's the big deal about predestination if it isn't about my pre-destiny?

Predestination! Now there's a hairy subject. Try to discuss this subject with a friend or two and see how it turns out? Good luck with that. They say fools rush in where angels fear to tread, so I'm going to put on my fools cap and give it a try.

Why would I want to do that—because any discussion of destiny must include God's pre-determined will for us? Your personal destiny grows out of the pre-destiny God has planned for you; which of course brings up the issue of our own free will to choose our destiny. A casual glance at this complex idea will tell you that it cannot be both ways. We cannot be free to choose if our choices are totally predetermined by the sovereign choices of God. Right? Well maybe there is more to this than meets the eye.

Predestination Puzzles

Wiser men than I have queried over this for centuries. How can we humans have free will and still be "under the thumb" of a no questions asked, no holds barred Deity like we see in the Bible. God is revealed to us in the scriptures as a heavenly Father who has plans for His family. Not only does He have plans, He has the power to make His plans come to pass. The question becomes,

"Can we as His children refuse to obey, hinder and prevent God's destiny for us?" Just read your Bible and you will clearly see that IS the biblical story! God has a plan and it seems to not be working because He has some very rebellious kids! Israel is God's chosen people and much of Israel's story is about its continued rejection of God's will and purpose. Even some very godly men, like King David, whom scripture calls a "man after God's own heart," often go astray. So, my question is probably your question, "if my life is already predetermined and predestined why worry about destiny, or even try to figure it out?"

God's Will

The Bible has much to say about the will of God. This is destiny language but spoken in "bible speak." It helps me to better understand God's will and destiny by seeing it from three viewpoints:

God's Intentional Will

We can view this as *God's perfect will*. His perfect plan for humanity is for His goodness to be bestowed on all men. God desires all men to be forgiven, and restored to fellowship with him. 2nd Peter 3:9 says it plainly, *"The Lord is not slow in keeping His promise, as some understand slowness. He is patient with you, not wanting anyone to perish, but everyone to come to repentance."* God's intention is to have all of us in His family. That's His destiny purpose for all men. As you well know there are some really bad apples in God's barrel.

Some men and women are so bent on evil they will die without God's forgiveness; not because He did not offer it, but because they did not want it or seek it. In their case God's intentional will was not fulfilled. Their destiny became their destination. Rejecting grace they receive wrath.

God's Circumstantial Will

We can view this as *God's permissive will*. This is His plan altered by our human free will. Romans 8:28 states it, *"and we know that in all things God works for the good of those who love Him, who have been called according to His purpose."* You have seen this in your own life. While you were making lemons—God was making lemonade. You and I have seen God's hand directing our steps, turning our foul ups into step ups. He is at work behind the scenes in the midst of our circumstances, even orchestrating them for our good and His purposes. Can you see in this that even our sins and rebellion are pre-known by God and somehow included in His pre-destiny purposes for us? He permits but He also persists! Amazing isn't it. Later we will see how failures are re-directed to fulfill our destiny.

God's Ultimate Will

We can view this as *God's* final Will. When the Lord Jesus was teaching his disciples how to pray, He told them to address their Father in Heaven and ask for *"thy will be done on Earth as it is in Heaven."* That day is coming. God the Father will have His way. The kingdom that was lost in the Garden of Eden, He through His determined purpose will restore. I'm thinking what that means is that even though we have free will and can miss our calling, purpose and destiny; God will have the last say! This is as true on a personal level as it is on a global level. His purposes to us seem flexible, changing, and even a bit controlled by human behaviors and decisions. Don't you believe it! All is not as it seems. You and I are not in control, it just appears that way at times. The hymn writer said it well:

> *This is my Father's world. O let me ne'er forget*
> *that though the wrong seems oft so strong, God is the ruler yet.*
> *This is my Father's world: the battle is not done:*
> *Jesus who died shall be satisfied,*
> *and earth and Heav'n be one.*[1]

A Difficult Equation

My personal understanding of God's pre-destiny for us has been aided by analyzing it as an equilateral triangle standing on three legs. By definition, an equilateral triangle is a triangle with three equal and congruent sides, all at a 60 degree angle. The Bible gives each of these three equal sides a name:

DESTINY: YOU AND GOD

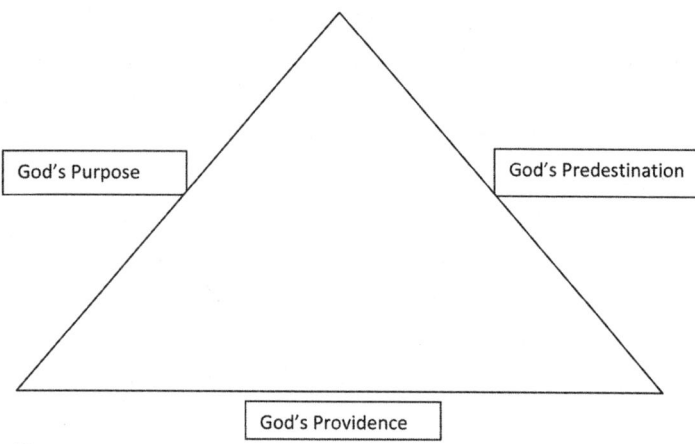

A triangle diagram with "God's Purpose" labeled at the upper left, "God's Predestination" at the upper right, and "God's Providence" at the bottom.

God's Purpose

> "And we know that God causes all things to work together for good to those who love God, to those who have been called according to His purpose."[2]

> "Just as He chose us in Him before the foundation of the world, that we should be holy and blameless before Him. In love He predestined us to be adopted as His sons through Jesus Christ, in accordance with His pleasure and will…according to His eternal purpose which He accomplished in Christ Jesus our Lord."[3]

God's Predestination (I prefer to call it "pre-destiny-ation')

> "For those God foreknew He also predestined to be conformed to the likeness of His Son, that He might be the firstborn among many brothers."[4]

> "But we speak God's wisdom in a mystery, the hidden wisdom, which God predestined before the ages to our glory"[5]

God's Providence

> "And those He predestined, He also called; those He called, He also justified; those He justified, He also glorified. What, then, shall we say in response to this? If God is for us, who can be against us?"[6]

DESTINY: YOU AND GOD

Purpose

When we consider predestination as an equal sided triangle it allows us to see our free will working within the framework of our Father's previously thought out destiny for us. There is a progression and a balance to this equation. First we need to understand God's purpose for us. Our personal history as well as mankind's history is continually shaped by God's purpose. God's big story will always intrude into our little story. His perfect will is for all men to enter his redemption in Christ. Sometimes I hear folks say that they are worried that some people are pre-destined to be lost and others pre-determined to be saved—like we are mindless automatons. Get this in your head and heart—predestiny is not about the lost. It is only about those who enter God's big story through their faith in God's son Jesus Christ. There is not one single hint in scripture that God has any pre-disposition toward humanity other than to father us and forgive us. Jeremiah says, *"for I know the plans I have for you, declares the Lord, plans to bless you and not to curse you, plans to give you a future and a hope... you will seek me and find me when you seek me with all your heart."* [7] The biblical message is that many are called, but few are chosen.

Did you notice that Romans eight says *"those who are called according to his purpose;"* they are the ones pre-destined. This entire destiny journey is not about lost humanity; rather it is about believers in Christ Jesus. Nowhere does scripture describe damnation for unbelievers as "pre-destined." God's purpose is salvation for all. *"This is good and pleases God our Savior, who wants all men to be saved and to come to knowledge of the truth."*[8]

The message is clear that God calls all men to join Him in restored fellowship; this is His only "will" for mankind.

God's Call and our Free-Will

Amazingly, when God does call us to salvation and we "choose" to believe, it feels like you are in charge. It feels like we sought God and we decided to repent and believe. Friend, it may feel like it, but how it feels and how it really is are not the same thing. I once read somewhere that when we stand outside the Gates of

93

Heaven seeking entrance, we look up and the sign over the pearly gates reads, *"Whosoever will may come."* Yet when we enter Heaven through those gates and look back, the sign reads from the inside. "Elected, Chosen, Predestined." From our earthly perspective we see our free will, but from the eternal viewpoint we were chosen from eternity past.

Pre-destiny-ation

Side two of our equal sided triangle is God's pre-determination to carry out His purpose (will) to save us.

Romans 8:29 reads, *"For those God foreknew he also predestined to be conformed to the likeness of His Son…"*

I love the Williams translation of this verse. *"Those He set His heart on beforehand, He marked off as His own to be made like His Son."* There can be no doubt about God's purpose—He wants to restore us to the stature Adam had in the Garden. God wants to conform us to Christ likeness and bring many sons to glory. In a later chapter we will see of what that "glory" consists. Rest assured—we are destined for glory, and it will truly be glorious! The exciting part for me is that God has already planned it out. It is pre-planned, and we therefore are pre-destined to fulfill God's purpose. One thing you see repeated over and over again in the Biblical narrative is that God plans His work then works His plan. The Bible describes God's determination to fulfill His purpose as God's "faithfulness." Repeatedly the biblical writers declare *"great is thy faithfulness."*[9]

Knowing and Willing

Notice again that it is those God the Father "foreknew" that He pre-destined. The implication here is not just that God is omniscient (all knowing) but rather that God has those chosen ones that *"He set His heart on beforehand."* How does God's knowing beforehand affect our destiny? Understand this—what God knows and what God wills (determines) are not identical; they are completely different. To know a thing is informational, but to will a thing is causal. Knowing in advance that a thing is going to happen does not cause it to happen. Right? What God knows and what God causes are not the same. For example, God knew before He created Adam and Eve that they would rebel and sin against His love. God did not cause them to sin, Adam chose of his own free will to sin. I learn from this that God knows before we are born whether we will be saved or not; then He exerts His will toward those who he foreknew would accept salvation. His will gets behind His purpose based on His foreknowledge. HE WILL MAKE HIS PREDESTINED ONES TO BECOME LIKE JESUS! NOTHING CAN EVER STOP HIM FROM ACCOMPLISHING THIS PURPOSE!

Israel and the Messiah

A clear example of this is God's relationship to His Son Israel. Israel failed God's purpose by rejecting their Messiah and our Savior-Jesus. What Israel, as God's Son failed to do, God accomplished in another Son of David—Jesus. God knew before Israel became a nation that they would fail their calling; but it was God's pre-determination that willed His purpose to be accomplished in Christ. In spite of Israel's failings, Christ came and died for our sins.

Providence

Side three of our destiny triangle is God's providence. Can you see God's providence as His determined activity in human affairs to fulfill His perfect will? What God purposes, he wills to happen, and he provides for its fulfillment. *"If God be for us, who can be against us?"*[10] This is a rhetorical question that demands a shouting reply, *"nothing!"* God is FOR US whom He called and pre-destiny-ated. His being for us is His daily provision to assure that our destiny is fulfilled. God provides for those He knew beforehand would accept His call (purpose). He is daily active in our lives providing means whereby we can become like Jesus. He is *"working everything for our good."*

Get on the Airplane

I am desperate to make this teaching about "pre-destiny-ation" more practical. So I am giving you a visual aid that helps me put all this together. Suppose with me that an American Airlines flight 123 is scheduled to fly from Los Angeles International Airport @ 9am every day to JFK Airport in New York City.

DESTINY: YOU AND GOD

This AA airplane is pre-planned, pre-scheduled to make this journey every day. It was created as Flight 123 for the very purpose of flying to NYC. There are thousands of AA airplanes with different schedules, but this one is pre-destined to fly from LAX to JFK.

Suppose on July 4th of this year you decide to fly to NYC and you choose AA flight 123 to make the trip. You go online and you purchase a ticket on that flight for July 4th. Now if for some unforeseen reason you fail to board AA flight 123, it will leave without you. Your absence will not alter or detour the pre-destined plans and purposes for that airplane. However, if you use your ticket and get on that flight and sit down in your pre-assigned seat, then that airplane will take you to NYC. Once you get on that airplane—then everything that is true about AA Flight 123 and its schedule and destination becomes true of you sitting in your pre-assigned seat. You are on your way to New York!! The airplane's destiny and destination have become your destiny and destination.

Do you see the analogy? God's pre-planned purpose for humanity is that AA Flight 123. See that flight as His perfect will. He wants us all to use our ticket and get on board. It is the good airship Salvation. Your ticket to ride is faith in Christ. When you become a Christ-follower, God puts you on the airplane. He has a special assigned seat just for you.

However, you must use the ticket to make the pre-destined journey; otherwise the flight will leave without you. God offers the ticket to everyone. It is a big airplane with room for all. Yet only those who board the plane make the journey. Only the God, who designed Flight 123, knows in advance who will use the pre-offered ticket.

So, when He calls you, get on the airplane!

DESTINY POINTERS:

1. You will find it helpful to not think of predestination as a doctrine to be understood so much as it is a truth to be lived out each day. What has God the Father already mapped out for me this day? That's a worthwhile question.
2. God provides for everything and everyone for whom He has purposes. You can ask for God's provision in each thing He

has purposed for you. Looking back at your life, can you see specific examples of God's provision?
3. You do not have to worry about the future. All you must do is walk in obedience to your present destiny. God will do the rest.
4. List three items that stand in the way preventing you from tuning into God's purpose for you. How many of these are emotional? How many are spiritual? How can you tear down these barriers?

CHAPTER ELEVEN

What a Difference a Day Makes

Meet Simon of Cyrene, you can learn from him.

We all have bad days when we cry out "why me Lord?" Caught up in the moment and it's agony we cannot see a bright tomorrow. We long to make some sense of it all. There are those times in life when today's clouds are so dark you cannot even envision a tomorrow. There is a destiny story in the Bible that speaks to this. Let me introduce you to a man of destiny who had a very bad day that turned out to be his best day.

Meet Simon of Cyrene

While reading through Mark's gospel I came across this sentence, *"and they pressed into service a passerby coming from the country, Simon of Cyrene (father of Alexander and Rufus) that he might bear his cross."* [1] This is a brief snapshot of a guy who was having a nice day that was badly interrupted. He was on vacation, a spiritual pilgrimage really, when he gets drafted into carrying the cross of a Roman prisoner. Because he was in the wrong place at the right time, his life is forever altered. We know by his name he is an African from Cyrene in Libya. Cyrene today is the modern city of Tripoli. Why is he, an African, in Jerusalem during the Jewish feast of Passover? A little research reveals some destiny clues! First there was a synagogue in Cyrene, where Jews worshipped. They had been transplanted there by the Greeks when they built the colony of Cyrene. Also, many Cyrenian Jews lived in Jerusalem and they had a large synagogue there. It would seem this *Simon of Cyrene* was an African Jew who has come to the Passover celebration. He is either a man of wealth or he has saved all his life to make this religious pilgrimage.

In three of the gospels scripture says that Simon was from the country, implying that he was not a local resident of Jerusalem. I tend to see it this way. Simon is on vacation, he and maybe his wife and kids (Alexander and Rufus) are walking through the busy streets of the city on a normal Friday morning. There is a commotion in front of them and crowds of people are gathering. Perhaps out of curiosity, this family rushes to see what is happening. Simon's spiritual journey is about to take a detour he could never have foreseen. The Bible says *"and he was pressed into service."* There's an understatement if I ever read one! Looking down the street, they see a badly beaten prisoner carrying a heavy wooden cross on his bleeding back. The prisoner, whom they will soon learn is Jesus of Nazareth, is having great difficulty walking with this burden on his shoulders. Jesus staggers and begins to fall right in front of them. Simon on impulse reaches out to catch him; when suddenly without explanation, a Roman guard seizes Simon's arm and pulls him from the mob. The guard demands Simon pick up the prisoner's cross and carry it for him to Golgotha, the place of execution. Simon resists, but to no avail, the guards *"press him into service."* If indeed his family is with him—they are stunned! A nice Friday morning has gone very bad, or so it seems. However, God is at work here. This is a "Kairos moment" for Simon and his family. They do not know it, feel it, or appreciate it, but God is in charge. What seemed then as a horrible experience, they will look back on in years to come as a destiny filled event.

Simon's sons Alexander and Rufus must have been young boys. Being impressionable lads you know they will remember this day all their lives. It was the day that dad carried the cross for the Son of God! I mention the boys, because it is Mark's gospel that reveals the clue to this destiny story. Why does Mark tell his readers that Simon is the father of Alexander and Rufus? None of the other Gospel accounts mention them. It seems Mark knew something about Simon that the others did not. In some important way, John Mark is telling us that this Simon of Cyrene had a future connection to Jesus and his followers. The plot "thickens!"

The Rest of the Story

This is getting fun. Think on this: Mark's gospel was first sent to Rome. The Apostle Peter was with the early church in Rome. Mark's gospel is really the gospel of Peter, because Mark wrote down the stories Peter preached and told. As Peter's traveling companion and later Paul's, John Mark had a connection to the Christians in Rome. Now it really gets interesting. When the Apostle Paul concludes his magnificent letter to the Roman Christians, he concludes the letter with various personal greetings. Romans 16:13 says, *"Greet Rufus, chosen in the Lord, also his mother and mine"*. Here Rufus is mentioned again!

Just maybe this answers the question why John Mark reminds us that Simon of Cyrene, drafted to carry the Cross for Jesus, is the father of Rufus and Alexander. Evidently John Mark knows Rufus and the remarkable story I am telling you. Furthermore, Mark's Gospel was first sent to the church in Rome. Are you connecting the dots with me? There is even more evidence that leads us to believe that Simon of Cyrene became a Christ-follower. Let's return to the scene of the crime (crucifixion).

Simon an Observer

Jesus walks ahead of the cross as Simon lifts the blood smeared cross to his broad shoulders. Jesus looks back at him from time to time, as if through his pain and fatigue, to silently say "Thank you." Along the mile or so walk through the narrow streets, the crowd increases to a frenzied mob. Carrying the cross behind Jesus, Simon is looking ahead at the battered and bleeding man struggling to walk in front of him. You can imagine the emotions of Simon and his family as they walk along slowly following Jesus.

They know who the Nazarene is—Jerusalem has been abuzz about him for days. What they do not know is why Simon is carrying his cross. It all seems so unfair, unexpected and dangerous. Will the Romans crucify Simon too? There are three prisoners in this gruesome parade; will Simon be the fourth? If indeed the wife and boys are following along that dark day, their hearts are fearful and anxious. After an hour of this torturous parade, the caravan of crosses reaches Calvary's hill. Upon command of the soldiers, Simon is told to lay the cross upon the ground, and then they rudely push him aside. Staggering back into the crowd, Simon finds his wife and sons. They grasp each other in a desperate hug. Tears are flowing, as they thankfully see that Simon is okay. But is he really? Their first impulse is to flee this brutal place, this execution ground, when Simon for some compelling reason halts and looks back. The family watches as cruel men pull Jesus down unto the cross. To their shocked dismay they hear the hammer and see the nails pierce the wrists of Christ. Drawn as if by a magnet, I imagine Simon and his family standing back a safe distance to watch the crucifixion of the man for whom Simon carried the cross. They hear him from time to time speak from the cross. Jesus asks for water, *"I thirst"* only to be given a vile drink which he refuses. Jesus speaks to a group of friends standing nearby saying *"John, behold your mother, mother behold your son."* We can imagine Simon and family staying there until afternoon when inexplicably the sky darkened as though heaven and earth were protesting. They hear Jesus cry out loudly, *"It is finished."* They watch Jesus die.

What just Happened

As Simon walks away with the crowd that afternoon, two women approach him and without an introduction touch his arm to say, *"Thank you for helping my son. May God bless you forever."* Simon's wife says to her, *"This Nazarene was your son?"* Mary looking back at her boy hanging dead on the cruel Roman cross says, *"yes, he is my son and He is God's Son too."*

Simon of Cyrene will be forever marked by this day's events. It is no accident that Simon and Jesus crossed paths, they have met in a destiny moment. My conjecture is that there is a connection between Simon of Cyrene and Simon who is called Peter. When Simon of Cyrene returns to his synagogue with his Jewish friends from Cyrene there is much discussion about all these events—the crucifixion, and Simon's strange part in the drama. Soon the whole city is whispering the rumor that Jesus has been raised from the dead. Eye witnesses are proclaiming this to be the greatest of all Christ's Miracles. There are rumors spread by Christ's enemies that his followers have stolen his body and spread the lies that Jesus is raised. These stories captivate Simon of Cyrene. They are the topic of discussion in his household. Could it be true? Could this man be our longed for, prayed for savior and Messiah? Could it really be true!

Two Simon's at Pentecost

The Jewish feast of Pentecost comes fifty days after the last Sabbath after Passover. It celebrates the giving of the Law to Moses centuries ago. However, this Pentecost will be like no other. As thousands of Jews from many countries are gathered in Jerusalem, Simon of Cyrene is gathered in the Temple area with friends and family. On this day another man named Simon, whom Christ-followers call Peter, stands on the Temple steps and begins to preach. His message is profound. He declares that Jesus, persecuted and delivered to the Romans by the Jewish leaders, is not dead. God has raised Him from the grave. Peter's message is that Jesus death was God's gift of forgiveness to all who will believe Jesus is the Christ (messiah). He has conquered death for all who will repent and believe this good news. We have good evidence that Simon of Cyrene may have been among those 3,000 who believed and were baptized that day. Acts 2 reads, *"Now there were Jews living in Jerusalem, devout men, from every nation under heaven... Egypt and the districts around Cyrene."* Peter preached his message of resurrection hope to Cyrenian Jews, some of whom were from the local synagogue. Many of them became Christ-followers and joined themselves to the new church in Jerusalem. Is it possible that Simon of Cyrene and his family became believers too?

Lucius and Simon Niger

Stay with me as I map a trail of evidence. We are following "crumbs" left on the pathway. Soon after Pentecost and the sudden explosion of the "Jesus movement" in Jerusalem, the persecution begins. The Christ followers are in peril. James, the brother of John the apostle is martyred. Many of the converts at Pentecost will naturally return to their homes, men like Simon of Cyrene. Others will migrate to other Roman colonies. Some converts from Cyrene go intentionally to Antioch.[2] In fact, years later when Saul and Barnabas are with the Antioch church (a city in modern day Turkey) there are two men from Cyrene mentioned as leaders in that church—Lucius and Simon who is called Niger. Now the nickname "Niger" can have two meanings. It literally means dark or black—as if to say this man Simon was a dark skinned man. It can also be a slang word for "African,' as if to say this man named Simon was an African from Cyrene (in Libya.) I feel like an investigative reporter. Are you seeing where this is going? Two men from Cyrene, Lucius and Simon called Niger are leaders in the Antioch Christian community. They are on the committee that sends Saul (who becomes Paul) and Barnabas on the first missionary journey. Could Simon who is called Niger be our man Simon of Cyrene who carried the cross for our Savior that day? If so, it amplifies the possibility that Rufus mentioned in Romans 16:13 is the son of Simon of Cyrene.

My Mother Too

Now we come to the true destiny conclusion to this remarkable bad day turned good. Who could have scripted this story except our heavenly Father? It is truly amazing. The final chapter in the mystery is found in Rufus' relationship with the Apostle Paul. When saying goodbye to the Roman church, Paul says two very revealing things in Romans 16; *"Greet Rufus, chosen in the Lord, also his mother and mine."* First Rufus' mom has become Paul's mother too! Paul is so close to this family that he can call Simon's wife his mother! Why does Paul need a mother? Because when

Paul became a Christ-follower his entire Jewish family disowned him. He is completely cut off from his Jewish family roots, only to have God provide a new Jewish-Christian family in Rufus and his mother. Secondly, Paul calls Rufus *"chosen in the Lord."* Now that's a rather strange way of describing Rufus as *"chosen in the Lord."* Which makes me wonder what was on Paul's mind when he describes his friend this way? He thinks of Rufus as *"chosen."* The word Paul uses here is the Greek word, *"eklektos".* This is a word frequently used to describe the destiny of Believers. To be chosen is to be elected by God to join His family and predestined purposes. Perhaps when Paul thinks of Rufus, he thinks of the boy from Cyrene whose daddy came to Jerusalem on pilgrimage, only to have their lives changed forever at the cross.

Find Destiny in your Day

Come to think of it—isn't that where each of us must come to find our destiny? I met Jesus at the cross and have been seeking to bear my own cross by His enabling Grace ever since. The lessons to be learned here are many, but the most important is that no matter how bad your day is or multiple days are, God has a plan and purpose at work for your good and the good of others through you. You just have to seek it, and walk in it by faith.

DESTINY POINTERS:

1. In what ways can you compare your life to Simons? In retrospect, can you see how God has been orchestrating your life to make you useful to Christ and His Kingdom?
2. Being a helper to Christ is a great privilege, like Simon we can help Christ carry His load. Have you ever asked Him how you can help? Have you done so recently?
3. Ask God to take a day (tomorrow?) and make it a day like no other. Step up your senses to become aware of what God places before you in each moment of that day.
4. When you have a "bad" day (in your opinion) ask yourself and God: "What is it you are teaching me in this moment and through this experience?"

Chapter Twelve

Men of Vision Fulfill Destiny

Plan your work, work your plan, but include your God given destiny.

It really is true that *"When God's man catches on fire, the whole world comes to watch Him burn."* Men and women who are visionary leaders draw a crowd. They become social and cultural magnets. This is especially true when the vision that possesses them is God given and destiny fulfilling. History repeatedly attests to how just one man or woman possessed of a visionary purpose can capture thousands and draw them into that vision.

The writer of Proverbs declares, *"Where there is no vision, the people perish"*[1] A more modern translation might be, "Where there is ignorance of their destiny, the people run wild." Just look about you at a world and cultures "run wild." If ever our world needed God driven visionaries it is now in the second decade of the twenty first century.

Vision and Destiny

Your vision makes God's destiny possible in your life and others. Without vision destiny does not often happen. Joel says in his prophecy, *"and it shall come to pass in the last days, that I will pour out My Spirit upon all mankind and your sons and daughters shall prophesy, and your young men shall see visions, and your old men shall dream dreams." (Joel 2:28)* Maybe we need to stop and define what we mean by a vision. I am using the word in the sense of a preferred future. Vision is foresight based on hindsight. Your vision becomes an informed bridge from the present to your future.

Almost thirty years ago I stood on a piece of ground in far north Dallas, Texas. It was more than a hundred acres of farmland with a small lake on it. A dear pastor friend of mine had stood on this spot and said *"Can you see it? I can see it! I can see a great Church built on this land. God has shown me this is where we will relocate Prestonwood church."* That was a prophetic vision that came true a few years later. Today, on the property, stands one of the great churches in America. Not just great in buildings of brick and mortar, but great in vision. My visionary friend "saw it before he saw it." That's what I mean by living your life in the grasp of a God given vision. Without a vision—people perish, but with a vision people flourish and destiny happens.

Visionary Leaders

Visions are used of God to set the direction of a person's life and move them into Destiny. The Bible tells many stories of folks like Joseph who see it before they see it. Joseph was a man of many visions; and his God given visions became God's plan and purpose for his family that eventually will become the nation Israel.

Samuel the prophet sees a King in a vision and obeying that vision Samuel finds the boy who would be king in the house of Jesse. That vision given to Samuel set the course of young David's destiny.

Jacob becomes "Israel" thru a vision.

Gideon finds God's will through visions.

Daniel the prophet sees visions of Israel's future that are still coming true today.

Joseph is about to wed Mary, only to be visited by an Angel who gives him an announcement of the Virgin birth and the baby's destiny.

The wife of Pontus Pilot has a vision and warns her husband concerning Jesus.

The Apostle Paul is given a road map of Macedonia in a vision

DESTINY: YOU AND GOD

that brings the Gospel to Europe instead of Asia. That vision changed the course of history.

Vision fuels Destiny

Men and women of vision change the world. The power of a God-given vision propels Destiny forward. Because God's anointing is upon it, and His purpose is behind it, our vision of a preferred future can and will shape Destiny. I often ask friends and others that I meet if they believe in destiny. Most people do. But if you ask them if they have a vision from God, you'll get another response—a blank look or puzzled stare! There is a breakdown somewhere. The same people who believe in the Bible stories of Daniel, Joseph, Paul and the prophets, have great difficulty accepting that they too can have a call of God that is visionary, extraordinary and unique. It is almost like we are too rational to be inspirational! Our tendency is to do one of two things with the idea of Vision:

First, we are afraid of any experience that we cannot reasonably explain. If someone tells me that God spoke to them in a dream or says, "I prayed for God's destiny to be revealed to me, and God showed me in a vision of what I am born to do," my immediate reaction is to raise a red flag! That's too way out there. I'm ready to run away or suggest we sit down and talk this through. Admit it; we are very leery of the *"God told me"* crowd. At least I am! However, is this a proper response—probably not? Caution maybe, but not rejection. How else are you and I ever going to hear God's voice, or find His heart for us? My best moments of direction and vision finding have come through prayer, surrender, and humbly seeking God's will.

This is the destiny implications of Proverbs 3:5-6 *"Trust in the Lord with all your heart and do not lean on your own understanding. In all your ways acknowledge Him and He will direct your path."*

This is wise counsel, because if you do not trust in the Lord you will not trust your vision as being from the Lord. Destiny is not found, achieved or fulfilled by advancing your own personal plans and ambitions. Many a man has wasted time and

109

money following his own plans and vision only to hit head-on into a brick wall when he discovered his planned future was not God's destiny-vision. When Paul is on trial before Roman rulers, Agrippa and Felix, he begins his defense by recalling his vision of Christ on the road to Damascus (Acts 9). Paul then confirms that the reason he is on trial is that *"I did not prove disobedient to the heavenly vision."*[2] That Damascus road experience forever changes Paul's destiny.

Secondly, we may take the opposite position by thinking that God only speaks to us in dreams, visions and in super extraordinary ways. This too is faulty. A God given vision can come to us through deliberate, thought out planning. It can come by listening to God through the reading of His Word and contemplating what He is trying to tell you. God may give you the inspiration as He often does, but He waits for you to believe it, work on it, and carry it through to completion. It may play out through circumstances, through people God places in your life or it may be even the "desires of your heart" God calls you to. Many a fulfilled vision came when someone prayed like it all depended on God, then worked like it all depended on them.

Your Vision

What is your God-given Vision? Ask yourself, "Am I captured by a vision that can determine both my destiny and my legacy? If you are not, you are missing God's potential for your life. I am audacious enough to say that God's Big Story is big enough to include every single one of His children in the drama. Your vision from God is your role in the play. How sad that millions have no vision beyond survival. They perish for lack of vision. Do not let that happen to you. Beyond survival is life abundant. There is significance in your future when you have a vision that can see it before you see it. Do whatever it takes to "hear from God." Seek His face and His pleasure upon your life. Destiny does not come your way by chance. It is worked out through being a person of faith who desires more than anything to please the Father. We need the attitude of Christ when He said, *"I do always those things that please the Father."* (John 8:29) That attitude is the pathway to fulfilled destiny!

Vision on Purpose?

Survival living is not purposeful living. Survival living is about existence, seldom about significance. This is why we see God continually giving vision to His children. The vision is the GPS that gives direction to our lives. The vision is "how we get there;" the "there" being your fulfilled destiny. When you have a vision you are inviting God to direct your steps.[3] I love the promise of Psalms 37:23, *"The steps of a man are established by the Lord; and He delights in his way."* That's exactly what you should be looking for—a life in which God delights in your way! The direction of our lives should not be determined by anything less than living out our vision. Why? Because your vision from God sets the direction for your preferred future, which has God's autographed signature written all over it.

Three Kinds—which Kind?

It has been said, "There are those who WATCH things happen; those who do not even know what's happening; and those few who MAKE things happen. The latter are the visionaries. You can easily recognize these leaders in politics, sports, science and the corporate world. In our ministry in Africa, where we are training young African leaders, I can illustrate it this way.

Wrong Jungle

Over a hundred and fifty years ago when the white man began to go "on Safari" in Africa he would hire perhaps 100 porters to carry the food, tents, and other necessary equipment for the journey. These porters had no idea where they were going. Each man picked up his load and followed the man in front of him. He would walk all day content to look at the back of the man in front. Yet, every Safari had a manager of the porters. This guy was in charge of the many details to care for those 100 porters. This manager's duty was to see that his men were properly fed, watered, and had the necessary things needed for the safari.

DESTINY: YOU AND GOD

He would give several men a panga (a long knife) so those in front could chop down brush and limbs when walking through the dense jungle foliage. This manager might even see that the pangas were sharpened daily to make the cutting easier. Also, every successful safari had a guide who knew the way to go. He was the leader. From time to time he might climb a hill or even a tall tree to see above the jungle. From his high advantage he could call down to the manager, "turn to your right, your men are chopping in the wrong direction." That surely is the difference between managers and visionaries. The manager stays busy with the details, but he cannot lead. Someone has to climb the tree and tell the group which way to go. Both are necessary, but only the leader truly sees the preferred future. He has a sense of destiny.

Vision and Limitations

Your vision limits your choices. It creates focus & meaning to your days. By this we mean, your vision tells your soul what is important. It is the small whispering voice that says to you, "don't major on the minors." Your vision is what you are really about every day all day. It should be your primary focus. The person who tries to do everything seldom does anything well. The leader cannot lead and sharpen pangas or direct traffic for porters. Visionless people are directionless people. They lack priorities and perspective. This is something of what Jesus meant when He admonished us to *"seek first the Kingdom of God and His righteousness, and all these (other) things shall be added unto you."*[4] *This* seeking the Kingdom means every day you are determined to live out your vision and destiny. So mark it well, when you ask God to give you His vision, be prepared to set some limits on yourself. The ugly trio of the world, the flesh, and the Devil will come daily to tempt and test you to detour from your calling. Satan did it to Christ in the wilderness and he will do it to you in your jungle as well.

Also, well meaning friends and family can distract you from your vision. They will not always understand you and your focus on your purpose. This happened to Christ when his mother

DESTINY: YOU AND GOD

and brothers came looking for him to urge him to return to the carpenter's shop because he was embarrassing the family name. Jesus stayed with his vision and calling, ignoring their request. The Jews certainly did not understand His vision and calling. They frequently thought they were right and he wrong; but Jesus had to be about His Father's business and you will too. This is why every child of God must personally "own" their vision. It came from God the Father as a gift to you. Now it is YOURS; you must take ownership of it. Otherwise it will never possess your heart and will. When you can say emphatically, *"this is my vision that will make me God's person I was born to be,"* then you are on your way to knowing clearly why you get out of bed each day! To fulfill destiny becomes your passion, and your vision is the GPS to direct your journey.

The Death of a Vision

Bill Gothard often spoke of how men of vision would be "tested." A dark time comes when you think the vision failed or you were wrong to think God gave it. You are *"in a pit with a lion on a snowy day"*[5] and you are not sure you should be in a pit with a lion on that particular day. In reading the biographies of so many great leaders you will see them have their doubts, fears and questions about whether they have really gotten their orders straight. Did God really give me this vision? Am I wrong about this? This is not working out like I planned! Good advice comes from Oswald Chambers who wrote, *"When God gives you a vision and darkness follows, wait. God will bring the vision He has given you to reality in your life if you will wait* on *His timing. Never try to help God fulfill His word* (to you)."[6]

I often think of the prophet Elijah sitting under a bush in the blistering desert heat hiding from Queen Jezebel.[7] He has forgotten Mount Carmel where just a few days ago he miraculously defeated and shamed the false prophets of Baal. His vision of a mighty God has been eclipsed by the vision of an angry mean woman! Jezebel has killed his vision of God. Elijah has "died" to the vision. His fear and depression have replaced faith and hope. That happens to most

113

of us who attempt great things for God. You will be tested! In those moments your "ownership" is coming up against your faith. Hang in there, if God be for us who can be against us! Jesus had a "death of the vision' moment on the Cross. His fearful soul cried out, *"My God, My God why have you forsaken me?"* He moved past the fear into faith and died in one of Destiny's finest moments saying, *"It is finished, into thy hands I commend my spirit."* (Luke 23:46)

A Death Sentence

It encourages me when men greater than I ever hoped to be reveal that they too struggle with faith.

That's why I appreciate the honesty of men like Paul. This man whom most consider to be the greatest Christ-follower ever, had his doubts and moments of almost caving in. When writing to encourage the Christians in ancient Corinth, Paul gives us a peek into his fragile psyche when he describes his depression as so deep, *"that we despaired even of life; indeed, we had the sentence of death within ourselves..."*[8] No one seems to know exactly what the great man meant by the words, *"sentence of death within ourselves,"* but the consensus is that Paul was so weary of the burden and vision God had given him that he had his moments of suicidal depression. Think about that will you! Paul had his moments of throwing in the towel. I can find hope in that. I am not the only one who has wanted to quit! Paul goes on to say that he found God's grace to be sufficient in all his trials. You and I can find hope in that same sufficiency.

You are your Vision

This is the remarkable thing about your God given vision. When you truly own it, it begins to own you. You not only possess a vision, it possesses you! People of destiny who impact their world for good and for God are single minded about it. Sure Paul got discouraged; it was because of his vision to take the Jesus message to the whole Roman world, that he was slandered, beaten, shipwrecked, jailed, and left for dead. You and I would get discouraged also. Yet, he was so captivated by his destiny

DESTINY: YOU AND GOD

vision that he can say to us, *'I press toward the goal for the prize of the upward call of God in Christ Jesus.'*[9] Our English word "scope" comes from the word "goal" that Paul uses here. The meaning is clear. He had the vision, the call of God, in his crosshairs. He is totally focused on it. He is single minded about it. And so are all those who fulfill God given vision. Their legacy depends on their focus; so does yours.

DESTINY POINTERS:
Some tips for finding your vision

1. *Report for duty*
When dealing with God, your availability is more important to him than your ability. 80% of fulfilling vision is just showing up!

2. *Surrender your future to God*
In this search for Destiny, it is better to surrender than to struggle. "Thy will be done" really works well in Kingdom economy.

3. *Pray and Fast*
Yeah, I know, too religious; right? Try it before you reject it. Pray and fast—put your focus on Him, not you.

4. *Spend time in the Word*
I know God still speaks in dreams and visions, but He has already spoken volumes to you in His Holy Word the Bible. Stick your individual nose in your individual Bible and prayerfully ask The Father to direct your steps.

5. *Seek wise counsel*
Get the opinions of Destiny minded Christ-followers. His Spirit is strong in them. They can inspire you.

6. *Be open to a prophetic word*
Yes, God may speak a word to you through Scripture, a sermon, a song, or a walk in the woods. He has a clear voice and you'll recognize it when you hear it.

7. *Examine your life-circumstances*
   When seeking a life-vision, it might help to be a bit practical. God doesn't call a blind man to be an astronomer, or a tone-deaf person to be a musician. He leads you where your skills and abilities can be enhanced and used of His grace.

8. *Walk in faith as God directs your steps.*
   Put feet to your prayers, fulfilling vision is a walk, a journey, and a pilgrimage. One day at a time!

Chapter Thirteen

Your Destiny Can Be Your Legacy

Your legacy should not be an afterthought when you live life on purpose.

The end result of fulfilling your God given destiny is that your life will count for something. You will have made a difference. You did not just take up space on this planet while you were here. You did more than just consume—you were a contributor. There is nothing worse than being a saved soul and having a wasted life. My greatest fear is to have lived my life and come to the end and realize I failed to live my life. To look back over the years and be ashamed I did not leave this world a better place than I found it; that would be a tragedy. Even more than that, I want to leave a legacy that inspires others to fulfill their destiny.

Two kinds of Legacy

There is a secular legacy and a sacred legacy. Your secular legacy is temporal and will pass away. It is made of those things that moth and rust will ultimately destroy. Your sacred legacy is as eternal as the Kingdom of God and never passes away! Some very fine men have been philanthropic and left the world with wealthy legacies that promote education, the arts, music, medicine, and such. As good as these legacies are—they are secular and not eternal. A sacred or spiritual legacy has God's destiny all over it. It is infused with destiny and timeless big picture reality. Sacred legacy advances the King and His Kingdom. Like waves upon the seashore it keeps on blessing and blessing. Unlike a secular legacy that may advance mankind, technology, or human culture, a sacred legacy advances the kingdom of God and blesses us eternally. William James said, "The great use of life is to spend it for something that outlasts it."[1] This especially applies to those of us who are Christ-followers. For us our true legacy will be measured by how we were connected to God's story.

Chain-link Legacy

The story has often been told of the mysterious legacy chain passed down from one ordinary man who touched the lives of several extraordinary men. The remarkable legacy chain begins in 19th Century Boston. The year is 1855.

Edward Kimball, a Sunday school teacher of high school age boys enters the Holton Shoe Store. He is not there to buy shoes; he has come on another mission. In the back room this teacher finds Dwight L. Moody, age 18, stocking shoes in his uncle Holton's store. That day, a day of destiny, Edward Kimball leads young Moody to faith in Christ. Dwight Moody, who only had a fifth grade education, goes on to become the great evangelist of the 19th century. Moody's evangelistic work on two continents, his founding of the great Moody church and the Moody Bible Institute are legendary.

Though uneducated, his charisma was electric. While preaching in England Moody met the brilliant Baptist pastor F.B. Meyer. Meyer invited Moody to preach a series of meetings at his church in York. This congregation of refined, educated Brits did not warm to Moody's rough, crude preaching at first. Although F.B. Meyer would become a life-long friend of Moody, he initially regretted he had invited D.L. Moody. He mistakenly judged the book by its cover! Two events would change F. B. Meyer forever.

Among those Moody touched was a wealthy lady Sunday school teacher in Dr. Meyer's congregation. She boasted to

DESTINY: YOU AND GOD

Moody, that all her ladies in her class were Christians. To her surprise, Moody challenged her to go outside the walls of the church and reach the lost women of York. Deeply touched by Moody's challenge she did just that! Later she thanked her pastor, Dr. Meyer, for inviting D.L. Moody.

Seeing how Moody's life and witness had changed this lady and the great anointing upon Moody's life and ministry; Dr. Meyer began his search for the deeper blessing of the Holy Spirit. In 1875, Moody spoke at a "Holy Spirit" conference in Brighton, England, that F.B. Meyer attended. Dr. Meyer became a great spokesman for the Higher Life Movement (later called the Keswick Convention). He began taking the message to North America. Preaching at Oberlin College, Ohio in 1886, Meyer met a young man named John Wilbur Chapman. Years earlier, Moody's personal counseling had inspired J. Wilbur Chapman to become a preacher. Chapman recorded being particularly impacted by Meyer's words, *"If you are not willing to give everything for Christ; are you willing to be willing?"* Dr. Chapman later said, *"That remark changed my whole ministry, it seems like a new star in the sky of my life."*[2]

Chapman, encouraged by Moody and Meyer became a very successful pastor and evangelist. Moody said of J. Wilbur Chapman, *"Chapman is the greatest evangelist of our Century."*

Are you seeing the chain link events that bring all these men together? It is a ripple effect. God is orchestrating all these destiny encounters. However, the story just gets better and better.

In 1893, J. Wilbur Chapman, now a very famous evangelist, needed a "front man" to promote his crusades. He hired a newly converted pro baseball player, Billy Sunday, at $40 a week. Greatly influenced by Chapman's preaching Billy Sunday slowly became an evangelist himself by preaching the sermons he had heard from J. Wilbur Chapman.

Although their preaching styles would become drastically different, Billy Sunday soon developed his own unique style of evangelism. Sunday became the most famous evangelist of the new 20th Century, preaching city-wide crusades throughout

119

DESTINY: YOU AND GOD

America. Sunday came to Charlotte, North Carolina for an evangelistic campaign in 1924.

And as a result of this highly successful campaign, a men's prayer group was formed that became the Charlotte Business Club. Ten years later, that men's prayer group was instrumental in bringing evangelist Mordacai Ham to the city. Now the plot thickens!

There was a young twenty something salesman/farmer in Charlotte, who delivered vegetables to town on his truck. Several high-school boys worked for him selling vegetables. When news of the 1934 Mordacai Ham campaign reached this young vegetable farmer, he wanted to take his teenage friends to the tent meeting. To entice a spirited young teen named William, he offered to let him drive the truck to the meeting.

So, off they went Al, William and his buddy T. W. Now, I've heard various versions of what happened that night, one that T.W. and Al sang in the choir and William stayed in the truck. Another version says they all sang in the choir. Anyway, that night or soon after both T.W. and William gave their lives to follow Christ. Their salesman/farmer friend Al was one happy guy!

You know the rest of this story. William is Billy Graham. His buddy is T.W. Wilson, who became Billy's companion in ministry for half a century.

I tell you this legacy story for several reasons. First, most Christians know of D.L. Moody, F.B. Meyer, J Wilbur Chapman, Billy Sunday, and Billy Graham. However, very few have heard of Edward Kimble, a Sunday school teacher in mid nineteenth century Boston. Even fewer of us know who the guy was who let Billy Graham drive his truck, just to get him to attend a Tent meeting. His name was Albert McMakin. Albert remained a friend to T.W. and Billy throughout his life. Without Edward Kimble and Albert McMakin there might not have been a Moody or a Graham. Their simple faithfulness to share the redemption message changed the course of history; and changed the eternal destiny of millions.

You Never Know

Secondly, the implication is clear; you and I can be difference makers too. God has always used ordinary people to do extraordinary things. Far too often I meet people who have no confidence that their life can make a difference. They feel small and of no consequence. I love the words of Betty Reese, *"If you think you are too small to be effective, you have never been in bed with a mosquito."* Well, we have all been in bed with a mosquito—at least I have in my travels to Africa. One pesky insect buzzing in your ear can make a huge difference! That's why I tell you again and again, God uses the ordinary to do the extraordinary. I need to believe that and so do you. Even today, you might meet someone who is lost to life and destiny. One kind word, one cup of cool water given in Christ's name and you are used of God to recruit a mighty warrior for the fight, or a saint for the cause. You just never know! There are so many folks who in a destiny moment, crossed my path, and God used me to speak truth into their lives. Some of those folks have developed into giants for God, extraordinary in every way. You just never know.

Each of us as Christ followers can make those ordinary daily decisions to follow God's leading and when we do we then enter into the bigger destiny picture. We are shaping our legacy almost every day. Hopefully you have learned that your purpose in life is not just to be happy – but your purpose is to *matter*, to be productive, to be useful, and to have it make some difference that you have lived at all.

If you live long enough, you will begin to see the impact your life is making on others. As I have aged and spent nearly half a century living out God given destiny, I can testify to the fact that God uses ordinary people to touch the lives of those who become extraordinary culture changing agents. Often we see only the moment or the momentary. We see the snapshot, God sees video. Our job is to show up, stand up, and speak up. I have often thought that leaving an eternal legacy is mostly about simply reporting for duty. When we show up, God shows up in us and through us.

He Still Speaks

Hebrews chapter eleven is a favorite to many. Here is God's Hall of Fame. The mighty destiny heroes are listed in this adventure narrative. I love Hebrews 11:4, *"By faith Abel offered to God a better sacrifice than Cain, through which he obtained the testimony that he was righteous, God testifying about his gifts, and although he is dead, he still speaks."* Heroes leave a legacy; though dead, they can still speak. I really like that! It challenges me to live my life in such a way that my life can still speak life into others long after I am gone. There are many, many examples of men and women whose life-message has left us with a legacy.

John Bunyan lived in 17th Century England. A prolific writer, his nonconformists ways landed him in the Bedford jail at age 32. Although truly innocent of any real wrongdoing, the authorities left Bunyan in jail for 12 years! That's right—12 years for just being a Bible preacher and writer. While in jail he wrote what was to become his spiritual autobiography, Grace Abounding to the Chief of Sinners. Today that work ranks with the Confessions of St. Augustine as a classic among spiritual journals. After being released from Bedford Jail, Bunyan had a period of great success as a preacher and teacher. Large crowds came to hear him speak. However, in 1676, John Bunyan was imprisoned again—being charged with "nonconformist teachings." This six months imprisonment in the small bridge jail over the river Ouse was a turning point in Bunyan's life. In those months of seeming despair, came forth perhaps Christendom's finest work—Pilgrims Progress. Who can doubt that Bunyan never planned his legacy from jail, yet it was to take place right there in that jail. Though dead—he still speaks!

Martin Luther was a very determined and courageous man of faith. His spiritual legacy is strong, an inspiration to millions. Yet one of Luther's greatest accomplishments came in a one year span of time while hiding from authorities. In 1520, the Roman church excommunicated Luther and branded him an outlaw. He was secluded for many months in the Wartburg Castle, disguised as a knight. While there Martin Luther translated the New Testament

DESTINY: YOU AND GOD

into German from the Latin, and during that troubled period wrote words and music to this poem, destined to become the stirring hymn *A Mighty Fortress is Our God*:

> *A mighty fortress is our God, a bulwark never failing;*
> *Our helper He, amid the flood of mortal ills prevailing:*
> *For still our ancient foe doth seek to work us woe;*
> *His craft and power are great, and, armed with cruel hate,*
> *On earth is not his equal.*

> *Did we in our own strength confide our striving would be losing;*
> *Were not the right Man on our side, the Man of God's own choosing:*
> *Dost ask who that may be? Christ Jesus, it is He;*
> *Lord Sabaoth, His Name, from age to age the same,*
> *And He must win the battle.*

> *And though this world, with devils filled, should threaten to undo us,*
> *we will not fear, for God hath willed His truth to triumph through us:*
> *The Prince of Darkness grim, we tremble not for him;*
> *His rage we can endure, for lo, his doom is sure,*
> *one little word shall fell him.*

> *That word above all earthly powers, no thanks to them, abideth;*
> *The Spirit and the gifts are ours through Him Who with us sideth:*
> *Let goods and kindred go, this mortal life also;*
> *The body they may kill: God's truth abideth still,*
> *His kingdom is forever.*

Luther would live to see this hymn become the national anthem of the German reformation. Though he is now dead, he still speaks.

Oswald Chambers died in 1917, a relatively young man at age 43 from complications of an appendectomy while in Egypt. He was there serving the British troops as a Chaplain. Chambers did not accomplish much in his short life other than being a seriously devoted Christ-follower. After his death, his wife Biddy returned to London where she painstakingly transcribed her shorthand notes of Oswald's sermons and devotionals into proper English. Ten years later, she published her late husband's notes as the book, *My Utmost for His Highest*. Two generations later, millions are still reading Chambers' works. He still speaks!

C.S. Lewis, is another one of those special men whose writings are his legacy. Although Lewis wrote brilliant novels such as, Lion, Witch, and the Wardrobe, The Problem of Pain, along with many other notable works, the amazing story is the origin of his most famous book. In the midst of a terrible war, C.S. Lewis was asked by the BCC radio to do a lecture series, which he did from 1941-1944. Later these lectures were put in book form and were released as three pamphlets. However, God had other plans for those apologetics. When later released in one volume as Mere Christianity, the legacy began. Millions have been touched by these lectures as both believers and unbelievers read its timeless message. Though dead, he still speaks!

Amazingly, as I think about the kind of destiny living that makes a difference, a daunting truth strikes me—you cannot really plan a legacy. You can live purposefully and intentionally, but you cannot assure you will leave a great legacy. If you were to ask C.S. Lewis, Oswald Chambers, or any other greats in God's Hall of Fame if they were surprised by the impact of their lives on others, I think they would say "I'm shocked" or "I never could have imagined what God would do with my words or life-message."

You Cannot Plan it

Legacy can be dreamed about, hoped for and even planned but the end result is up to God. Really, all any of us can do is to give it our best shot—everyday. Legacy is built upon the tiny bricks of daily decisions and faithful devotion to God's high calling. It is built one day at a time, living out your destiny moment by moment. Legacy grows out of the soil of your obedience to what God has been doing in your life. It emerges out of the stuff of Destiny. As you allow God to direct your steps, those steps lead to a tower of spiritual legacy left behind you as a monument to God's glory. Surely the bravest and most noble among us are those fine souls who live for eternity and have the clearest vision of what is before them, glory and danger alike, and yet notwithstanding, go out and meet it. Those are the folks who, though not seeking it; find it. They will make their mark, leaving a sacred legacy.

> "In youth because I could not be a singer,
> I did not even try to write a song;
> I set no little trees along the roadside,
> Because I knew their growth would take too long
> But now from wisdom that the years have brought me,
> I know that it may be a blessed thing
> To plant a tree for someone else to water,
> Or make a song for someone else to sing."
> *Author unknown*

DESTINY POINTERS:
How to leave a Sacred Legacy

1. Enter into God's Destiny for you at this moment in time. Give yourself to fasting, prayer, and brokenness before God.
2. Begin each Day to live your life on purpose, His purpose for this day. Pray to have a sensitive heart that will be on the lookout for those serendipity Destiny moments God is placing in your path. Don't just count your days, but make your days count!
3. Purpose to do loving acts to others that fulfill your destiny. Be alert to those destiny moments God brings your way.
4. Know that your legacy is growing moment by moment day by day—you cannot see it or even feel it, but it is being stored up in God's vault.
5. Think about destiny, forget about legacy—just let it happen.
6. At the end of a week—check your heart. Did you live out your Passion in some significant way?
7. Know this truth—Destiny lived out and legacy fulfilled will be rewarded with Crowns and our Savior's "well done my Child!"

CHAPTER FOURTEEN

Who You Are and Who You Really Are

Sons of God are destined for greatness.

Discovering your destiny shouldn't be that complicated—but it is! When I have asked my friends this pointed question, "Are you living out your destiny?" they look at me like a calf staring at a new gate. It just isn't a question with which we are comfortable. Maybe if I rephrased the query it would help: "are you fulfilling God's purpose for your life?' Oops! There it goes again—same look! You see, the amazing thing is we all desperately want to live a life that really matters, but just how to get there, that eludes us.

Desires

Here is a much better question, "Why would our heavenly Father create us to fulfill our destiny and then make it as difficult as a treasure hunt?" What would you think of a parent who tells his child, *"I love you and want you to be happy. I have a detailed plan already laid out for your future success. I have it all written down for you; all you have to do is find it. Oh by the way, I've put my plan for you in an envelope and hidden it away. It won't be easy for you to find, and it may take you a lifetime to do so. I have made it difficult so you'll appreciate it when you finally do discover it."* You see my point? I don't think our loving Father/God wants us to waste our lives desperately looking for a purpose driven life! No, never! He does not want us to waste even a day outside His will. The secret to our destiny and purpose is found in our basic God designed personality. He knit us in our mother's womb. So let us begin in two directions looking for destiny. First look at your passions and fundamental desires.

DNA and Desire

A few years ago I was impressed by John Eldridge's fine book, *Wild at Heart*. Eldridge wrote this book to help men discover their destiny through their "maleness." He asserts that we humans, created in God's image, have in our DNA traces of God's own DNA. For example, there are both male and female attributes in the character and personality of God as revealed to us in scripture. God is a Father, but He is also a warrior. God is fierce and will pick a fight with His enemies. God is goal oriented, determined, dependable, and a strong tower. You be the judge—do these attributes reflect maleness or femaleness? That's easy, right? Also, God is merciful, kind, compassionate, and an encourager. Which does that sound like—your dad or your mom? So, the first clue to our destiny is found in our maleness and femaleness. Men and women are passionate about different things. We are different from birth. God created us that way. This is easily demonstrated by observing children at play. Just go to a children's nursery and watch the toddler boys doing their thing. The boys are running, jumping, wrestling, and competing. Now observe the sweet little girls—what are they about? They are busy talking, relating, helping, and loving. Boys love action, girls love connecting and discussing.

What are you passionate about?

My strong hunch is that men are more like Father God than Mother Nature. Before our mothers, sisters, wives and a feminized culture tried to tame us, we men were made by God to be warriors, fierce, competitive, protective, strong and very courageous. The Bible says to men, *"Act like men, be on the alert, stand firm in the faith, be strong. Let all you do be done in love."*[1]

DESTINY: YOU AND GOD

Men, our maleness is a resource and indicator of our destiny. If you have read *Wild at Heart*, you will remember Eldridge affirms that real men are passionate in three areas:

We are looking for a battle to fight
We are searching for an adventure to live
We want a woman to rescue

Think about it. Men care deeply about those three areas. They define us. We men want a battle to fight; that means we are warriors at heart and are cause and action oriented. Men want to do something, not just talk about it. We men love an adventure. We want a battle that has some risk involved. Finally, we want to be some lady's hero. We want a woman we love to be proud of us. Amazingly when God's man finds his battle, he willingly pursues the adventure without assessing the risk, and he very much wants a woman to be proud of him for where his destiny led him. These manly desires are revealing clues to our destiny.

Ladies are Destined too!

Lest I leave you ladies to assume only males have Godly instincts, let us affirm that God has a feminine spirit as well as a warrior spirit. In fact, those descriptions of the Holy Spirit throughout the scriptures all speak of a female heart. The Holy Spirit is loving, kind, joyful, peaceful, patient, and gentle.[2] To my way of thinking, women are created in the image of God's "feminine side" if such an idea can be entertained without too much controversy. Being created for mercy, compassion, faithfulness, and understanding, any woman can find destiny in following your heart in those areas that are your core being. As in any thing there are exceptions to the rule. There are culturally modified females who are competitive, fierce, or none nurturing; even as there are so called "soft" males who are not fierce or strongly competitive. What is true is that male and female are fundamentally different because God made us so. To deny this is to miss fulfilling destiny in a joyful and meaningful way.

Desires and Personality

Who you are was basically determined before you were born. God "formed you from your mother's womb."[3] We often confuse personality with temperament. Your personality can be cultured, developed, refined, or even altered; however your temperament is like your psychological DNA. Your temperament is YOU, the real you that God created for His purposes. Knowing your temperament is important because it is a sign post to your passions and desires.

Being born an introverted person is not a limitation, unless you spend your life trying to be an extrovert. Extroverts get their energy from people; they love to be in a crowd or group. They do not do well alone. Conversely, introverted people get their energy from solitude; they refill their empty tanks by being alone. Put an introvert in a crowd and he'll soon run out of energy and go find a chair and a magazine to read!

These are destiny indicators. God uses these temperament traits to lead us into predestined roles He has chosen for us in the big drama. God normally does not call a deaf or muted person to be an opera singer nor does he call a rigidly structured temperament person to be an innovative entrepreneur. His callings are in line with His creation.

Talents and Temperament

Do not confuse talents or abilities with your basic temperament. We all have known highly successful people who have overcome lack of talent by sheer force of will and determination. I have known several preachers who stutter when in normal conversation, but when preaching or praying, they seldom stutter. We have also known really talented entertainers or preachers who by temperament were introverts. Introverts can perform for the crowd but it exhausts them. They have developed their skills to perform but it does not energize them as does solitude. Talents and abilities can be developed and made extraordinary by repeated use; but one's God given temperament is your design made by your designer. Your temperament is where your heart is, it is where you get motivated and energized. This may explain why some introverts who become public speakers, actually do their best legacy work being alone writing a book. What I am saying is that their speaking may be their career but their destiny is elsewhere.

So, the old admonition to "know thyself" is a good one. I spent too much of my early years trying to be what others said I should be. I was raised by women with no male mentor in my life. These dear ladies, mom, grandmother, and aunties, all tried their best to tame the wild boy in me. They almost succeeded, but thanks be to God, He sent "a few good men" into my life to initiate me into manhood.

Design

So, desire can definitely reveal your Design. Remember that God made you uniquely you; there is not another anywhere like you. You are fearfully and wonderfully made the Bible says. That means your desires do reveal your design and your design can reveal your destiny. God designed you for this time and place in history. That is why I strongly suggest you search your heart to find what you truly love and want out of life. Unless you have been twisted and warped by sin, prejudice or peer pressure, your heart's desires can show your design and destiny.

The Psalmist said it like this *"Delight yourself in the Lord; and He will give you the desires of your heart. Commit your way to the Lord, trust also in Him, and He will do it."*[4] These words are wise counsel. They are condition and promise. There is my part and there is His part. I meet His conditions and He always keeps His promises. Notice the two conditions—"delight yourself in the Lord." That is telling you to want God's will more than anything. Make pleasing the Father the delight of your soul. Secondly, *"Commit your way to the Lord."* That means you have chosen His way over your way or any way! When you can commit your way to God, you can trust Him to direct your steps—*"he will do it."* Friend, that's a really good deal. It is doable, because my heart's desires are a reflection of His design in me; and my discovered design can lead me to fulfilled destiny.

Spiritual Gifts

Without being too technical here, a truly wonderful part of a born-again Christian's "design" is his or her gifting. The day a person receives Christ as Savior and Lord, several really great things take place. First, becoming a Christ-follower puts you into God's destiny path. You are in the coach's play-book.

Secondly, being born of the Spirit means that Christ by His Holy Spirit has come to reside in you. He lives in you! When Christ came to dwell in you he did not come empty handed; He came bearing gifts—grace gifts. These gifts of the Spirit are supernatural Christ abilities that become an essential essence of your being. You are your gift; and your gift defines you and your destiny.

Let me explain what I mean. Even as I am typing this manuscript for you to read, Jesus Christ the teacher lives in me the writer. He is teaching you through me. My teaching gift is not really a natural talent I possess but rather a "Christ enablement" that possesses me. He gave me this gift the day He came to live in me. From that day until this day, I have been motivated to "stir up the gift"[5] that is within me. Over the years God's design in me and His teaching gift have directed my life towards being a Bible teacher and a mentor of men. Following my gift has shaped my destiny.

What is true of me is true of you as a Christ-follower. God's Spirit has gifted each of us in different ways as members of Christ's body, the Church. Simply put—discover your gift, know your temperament, follow your male or female instincts and you are on your way to fulfilling destiny.

There it is—desire indicates design and design equips for destiny.

Not so Fast

However, there needs to be an asterisk and a few footnotes applied here. Even with all these "clues" to common sense destiny living, I am reminded that Father/God is Sovereign; and only He knows the script of "God's Story." Paul reminds us that we cannot always predict what God will do or whom He will call. He writes to the Corinthians:

> *Remember, dear brothers and sisters, that few of you were wise in the world's eyes or powerful or wealthy when God called you.*

DESTINY: YOU AND GOD

Instead, God chose things the world considers foolish in order to shame those who think they are wise. And he chose things that are powerless to shame those who are powerful. God chose things despised by the world, things counted as nothing at all, and used them to bring to nothing what the world considers important. As a result, no one can ever boast in the presence of God.[6]

History has demonstrated repeatedly that God's ways are not our ways and His thoughts are not our thoughts. He chooses people we would never have chosen to accomplish His purposes. The Bible stories are all about very common, ordinary people that God predestined for greatness. Look at a guy like Moses. He is an outcast from both the Egyptians and the Hebrew slaves of his origin. When God called him out of the desert, Moses protests to God, "who am I to go before Pharaoh, I cannot even speak clearly—I stutter!" [7] I often think God has a good sense of humor! I know he does because He puts up with me! So do not lose heart. The callings and elections of God are sure—and they surely include each of us regardless of education, training, talent or charm. Eighty percent of the battle is won by just showing up. God specializes in our availability, not our ability.

DESTINY POINTERS:

1. Fulfilling your destiny can begin by asking yourself some basic questions. The first being, what do I really like to do, or what am I truly passionate about that can reveal destiny?
2. Your destiny is tied to your talents, desires, and temperament. Have you offered those to God as a living sacrifice to allow Him to get you going down destiny's path?
3. Have you ever tried to determine what your spiritual gifts truly are? Not what you want them to be, or think they should be but what they are evaluated to be? (see www.kodachrome.org/spiritgift/)
4. Every born again person has one or more spiritual gifts. These gifts are destiny markers God uses to accomplish His purposes

on the earth. Do you see God moving, anointing, and using your gifts? If not, why not?
5. On a scale of 1 to 10, just how available are you to the Holy Spirit?

Chapter Fifteen

Destiny Demands Defiance

A life worth living is a future worth fighting for.

Living out your destiny is seldom easy. It seems the world, the flesh, and the devil will come at you like a swarm of bees to drive you off your path to fulfilled destiny. Just ask any of God's heroes of faith if being all you can be for God is easy.

Ask Joseph as his brothers sell him into slavery and Potiphar (Pharaoh) puts him into prison for something he did not do. In spite of all his trials Joseph can say to his brothers some years later, *"What you meant for evil, God meant for good."*[1]

Ask John the Baptist if being a man of destiny was easy. From Herod's prison hear him ask his disciples to go question Jesus, *"are you really the messiah?"*

Ask Paul from his prison cell if being an apostle to the Gentiles was easy. He will tell you it was his destiny; but it came at great risk and personal sacrifice.

Ask Jesus if being the Savior of the world was without struggle. He will say, *"The son of man must suffer many things and be rejected…"*[2]

Taking Destiny by the Throat

One of the most remarkable statements Jesus ever made has

to do with fighting for your destiny. He said *"And from the days of John the Baptist until now the kingdom of heaven suffers violence, and violent men take it by force."*³ The kind of violence he speaks of is not physical malevolence but rather a defiant spirit that is willing to risk all to fulfill your destiny. Fulfilled destiny and a warrior spirit go hand in hand.

Simply put, often friends and foes alike do not understand us when our face is set upon doing the revealed will of God; that is why we must have the courage and commitment to fight for it. Most people of destiny have two striking qualities. One, they are for the most part misunderstood until history validates them. Two, they have to stubbornly resist being average to achieve the extraordinary. Dan Bailey says, *"Some succeed because they are destined to, but most succeed because they are determined to."* ⁴ I think it takes both destiny (a calling) and determination. Men and women of vision must have a defiant spirit to achieve destiny and leave a lasting legacy.

Pragmatism won't work

Often we look at our current circumstances and become totally discouraged. Despair gets in the way of destiny. Depression quenches the fires of inspiration. We cannot see how to get there from here. Beware of settling for less than your dreams. Pragmatism can blot out your dreams of a bright future. If you are not willing to fight for your destiny, you can miss it. Beware of those whispering voices that tell you to "just deal with it, make the most of it, or make lemonade out of lemons." That all sounds practical, but it will not inspire you to rise above and fulfill God's calling on your life. You can settle for mediocrity and miss the inspired calling God has for your life.

Looking back on my life, I am so grateful that I did not settle for being practical or pragmatic. I grew up with little hope of being anybody or doing anything of significance. Raised by a single mom who only had a high school education, I don't even remember meeting an adult in my early years that had a college degree. We were poor, blue collar, working class folks. Later when I graduated from college, I was the first to do so in our extended family of nearly

DESTINY: YOU AND GOD

100 people. There were times when my dream of being a preacher seemed so fanciful and farfetched. The "how" of it was huge, the possibility of it was miniscule. I remember at age sixteen telling my mother, "*Mom, God is calling me to be a preacher. I want to become an evangelist like Billy Graham.*" She was less than enthusiastic about that announcement; in fact she cursed me and told me to become a lawyer—that's where the money is! Now that's pragmatism at its finest! Fourteen years later my mom came to faith in Christ at one of my preaching missions. Her destiny was very much connected to mine. Believe me when I tell you, had I listened to her and several other practical suggestions from well meaning friends and family, I would not be writing this book. When it comes to destiny, you have to want it, believe in it, and defiantly fight for it."*The Kingdom of God suffers violence and violent men take it by force.* Your destiny is your high calling; it demands your utmost for His highest. [5]There is wisdom in the words of media giant Sumner Redstone, "*We all have to decide how we are going to fail; by not going far enough or by going too far."* Being pragmatic about God called destiny will guarantee you did not go far enough, reach high enough, or risk enough.

Passivity won't cut it

Another way to all but guarantee failed destiny is to be too passive about it. It is flawed thinking to assume that we are just pawns in God's hands and He is going to work out your life—regardless. If being a pre-destined child of God means I can go through life doing nothing expecting God to do it all, then I am seriously misreading scripture and history. When you read that Jesus, even though He is the Son of God, learned obedience from (through) the things which He suffered; [6] you can be assured God takes our obedience seriously. Being obedient to God's call is not to be mistaken for being passive. Destiny is worked out day by day through our obedience and faith in God's promptings.

The Church in Nazi Germany

Edmund Burke is quoted as saying, "The only thing necessary for the triumph of evil is for good men to do nothing." [7] This became

DESTINY: YOU AND GOD

vividly clear to me years ago when I first visited Krakow Poland during the Cold War. The year was about 1984. The Auschwitz death camp is next to the railroad in Krakow. One day I spent several hours touring the Auschwitz concentration camp; which is now a Holocaust Memorial. I was preaching in a small church in Krakow that week when the pastor and I got in a conversation about Auschwitz and the horrible things that happened there. To my surprise, this pastor had lived in Krakow during the Nazi occupation. I asked him if the residents of Krakow knew what was going on inside the walls of Auschwitz during those dark days of the War. Rather glibly he replied, "Oh yes, we all knew. Every day you could see the train loads of Jews being unloaded by the thousands. We could see and smell the smoke from the ovens." Somewhat taken aback, I asked him, "Did the Christians in Krakow do anything to stop the genocide?" To this day I can see him shrug his shoulders and say, "What could we do, it was too late, just too late."

It probably was too late. However the gripping truth is that the church in Germany was too passive about the rise of the Third Reich and the racial hatreds that brought about the Jewish Holocaust. Whether the church could have done more to resist, or even make a difference, will be the judgment of history. Only a few dissenting voices like Dietrich Bonhoffer (and about 600 others in concentration camps for opposing the Nazis) were willing to die rather than compromise. Where was the defiant warrior heart of the Church during the rise of the Reich? For the most part, the German church was too caught up in the politics of it all to voice a loud complaint.

The Bielski Partisans

Did you happen to see the film, <u>Defiance</u> starring Daniel Craig? I loved that movie—it is based on the true story of the Bielski Partisans—a resistance movement during the Nazi invasion of Poland. The Bielski families were Jews of Belarus, (Poland). The three Bielski brothers saw their parents and other family members murdered by the Nazis. Tuvia Bielski and his two brothers Zus,

DESTINY: YOU AND GOD

and Asael, formed a resistance group by hiding in the forest and refusing to yield to the Nazi occupation of Belarus. Eventually they saw their purpose for existence was to leave no Jew behind. Any Jew who cared to join them was saved. They took in women, children, the elderly and the sick. Any Jew who was willing to resist was welcomed. At war's end, over 1200 Jews of Belarus had been rescued. Today their descendents number over 10,000 souls scattered all over the world.

This remarkable story came to pass at great cost and effort of will. The Bielskis were warriors fighting not just for their personal survival, but more so for the survival of the Jewish people. They were willing to kill those who would exterminate them; and they did so often. For over three years they lived in the forests of Belarus hiding from the Germans and fighting to the death when necessary. If they had been passive, they would have all died by Nazi execution squads. Instead they were defiant and fought for their right to survival and destiny.

I see in the warrior spirit of the Bielski brothers what is needed in all those whom God will use to shape history and redeem mankind. You cannot live out your God given destiny without coming in conflict with your culture. Living out destiny requires a defiant warrior spirit. The Bielski Partisans resistance spirit is the 180 degree opposite of my pastor friend in Krakow who said, *"We knew, but what could we do?"*

Defiance of another Kind

Another kind of defiance was fought in England by William Wilberforce, Thomas Clarkson, William Pitt and others, when they were determined to abolish the slave trade. From 1785, the year of his conversion to faith in Christ, until his death in 1833; Wilberforce's name is forever linked to his determined fight against slavery. For 26 long and determined years he sought to enact laws in the British parliament that would abolish the slave trade. He met stern and malicious opposition from wealthy and powerful men who made a fortune from slavery. Wilberforce and Clarkson presented bills to parliament in 1791, 1792, 1793, and again in 1797, 1798, and 1799. Then again in 1804 and 1805 they presented more abolitionist legislation. All were defeated! Yet these culture warriors kept up the fight, never relenting.

During those hard years of fighting for abolition, William Wilberforce said, *"If to be feelingly alive to the sufferings of my fellow-creatures* (Slaves) *is to be a fanatic; I am one of the most incurable fanatics ever permitted to be at large."* [8] Although a minority most of his life, this really good man changed history when in 1807 the British parliament finally passed the Anti-Slavery Trade Act. Three days after his death in 1833; England abolished slavery in the Empire forever with the Slavery Abolition Act.

May Their Tribe Increase

A century ago, the destiny battle was to free the world of slavery. It took a long line of warriors and battles fought to change the culture of slavery. Men like William Wilberforce, Thomas Clarkson, Robert Moffat, David Livingston, Abe Lincoln, Martin Luther King, and Nelson Mandela all have a common characteristic—a spirit of defiance. Here we are over 100 years later, slavery is abolished and human rights are front and center worldwide. Today we have other culture battles that we are destined to fight. The world awaits other culture warriors who will fight the good fight. Those men were determined to bring about change in their generation. *"The kingdom suffers violence, and violent men take it by force"* (Matthew 11:12). What about your generation? Has God shown you the battle you are to fight? Are you willing to fight it? I pray so, because the Kingdom of God is made up of those who are willing to show up, stand up, and speak up. Destiny fulfilled does not come to you, you have to go get it and take it by the throat.

Lion Chasers

Mark Batterson has a great book I frequently recommend to men I am mentoring. It is entitled, *In a Pit with a Lion on a Snowy Day*. The book is based on an event in the life of Benaiah, one of King David's mighty men. Evidently this guy Benaiah was a real warrior, afraid of nothing. The Bible says of him, *"And Benaiah the*

DESTINY: YOU AND GOD

son of Jehoiada, the son of a valiant man, of Kabzeel, who had done many acts, he slew two lion like men of Moab: he went down also and slew a lion in the middle of a pit on a snowy day."[9]

Now I have to admit that in all my years of reading the Bible I had never noticed this sentence about David's body guard named Benaiah. He goes into a pit with a lion for the purpose of killing it—on a snowy day! Who is this guy? Is he crazy or what? He is not only a lion killer, he is a lion chaser. Instead of running from the lions, he runs after them. What's the point? Mark Batterson makes a very good point that all of us have lions in our lives that we run away from. They are the obstacles, barriers, and circumstances that keep us chained in fear, mediocrity or defeat. Then when God shows us a destiny opportunity, a calling, or a moment in life when we can make a difference, we need the defiant spirit to go down into that pit and show the lion whose boss! Even on a snowy day when it isn't comfortable to do so.

I am telling you this again so you'll hear it loud and clear. You must become a lion chaser; turning obstacles into opportunities. You must be strong, determined and very courageous. You will have to fight for what you want to achieve. God's enabling grace and the incredible power of His Spirit will sustain you as you walk by faith in His will. Those brave souls that shape history and get their name written in the Book of Life are those obscure body guards like Benaiah who chase lions for God.

DESTINY POINTERS:

1. Do you have a strong enough sense of Destiny to make you willing to fight for its fulfillment? What are the "desires of your heart" that have been placed by God that require you to be counter-cultural?
2. Would the words "risk taker" describe you? Or are you better described as "fearful" or "cautious"?
3. When you come up against obstacles, are you prone to quit,

or is there a lion chaser in you that will turn obstacles into opportunities?
4. Where in your culture do you see yourself being a culture changing agent?

Chapter Sixteen

The Risk of Reaching for Destiny

Believing all God has for you requires us to risk what only faith can see.

During the years that most of Eastern Europe was under the yoke of Communism, many Christians from the free West went in and out of those Eastern bloc countries doing ministry with oppressed Christians and churches. It was during those years that I and a few friends helped pastors in Romania, Poland, Serbia, and Czechoslovakia. These were difficult days and we had to be very careful while in those places as the secret police (called by various names in each country) were watching us and those we befriended. I personally felt a call of God to preach behind the "Iron Curtain." It became my destiny at that time in my life, so I did it fervently for several years.

Too Popular

As I went in and out of Romania in particular, preaching to large crowds in the dissident churches, my fame began to spread with both the churches and those watching us. While preaching in the largest church in all of Eastern Europe we were warned by friends that the police would arrest us if we continued. In January of 1984 while trying to cross the border from Hungary into Romania; I and two American preacher friends were turned away at the Romanian border. The Romanian authorities had my name and pastor Sam Friend on their "black list." We were not allowed entry. When the Immigration Police turned us away, by phone we called the church that was expecting us. Thousands were gathered for a week of revival and evangelism. I was the featured speaker. I remember telling Pastor Paul Negrutz: *"They have denied us entry, but we are coming, pray for us, we will find a way to enter Romania."*

New Passports

Turning our loaded van around was a depressing moment. The van was filled with medicines, food, and many other essentials for the poor Christians we were helping. We also carried several thousand dollars in our money belts to give for the support of struggling Romanian pastors. Sam and I pulled off the road in a small village near the border and prayed and planned. What to do? It became evident that we were denied entry because our passports had so many Romanian entry stamps (visas). It was a red flag to the border agents. So, Sam and I and the young preacher we had with us, Jon Randles, came up with "Plan B". We were about five hours drive from Budapest and the American Embassy there. At the Embassy we could get new passports—with no stamps in them! That's exactly what we did. The Embassy officials warned us about entering a Communist country where we were not welcome and tried to dissuade us. We were on a God given mission and felt we must at least try one more time. Before leaving the American Embassy we told them that if they had not heard from us by a certain day the next week; to come looking for us! Our plan was to drive south into what was then Yugoslavia (Serbia) then turn east and north to enter Romania from the Yugoslav border. Our hope was that new passports would fool the immigration police and that they would not be looking for us coming in from the seldom used Yugoslav crossing.

A very Cold January

No sooner had we left Budapest heading south than it began to snow. It snowed, and snowed, and really snowed for days

DESTINY: YOU AND GOD

on end! The temperature dropped into the teens (Fahrenheit). It became one of the coldest winter freezes anyone could remember; and here we were driving a Volkswagen van across mountains, over small roads with no chains on those small tires. It was a nightmare! Our first night we drove into a remote little village somewhere in northwestern Yugoslavia looking for a hotel room. The innkeeper looked at us with eyes as big as marbles—he had not seen an American since World War II! He asked us why we were here in his part of the world. We said we were tourists! That really made him blink! Tourists—yah right?

In Country—now what?

Traveling ever so slowly in the deep snow on roads with little traffic, we arrived at the Romanian border in late afternoon. With nervous anxiety and a prayer on our lips we waited as the Romanian border police checked us out. As if by God's grace, we were allowed to pass. Because there were no computers in 1984 the border guards had no information about us. We had outsmarted them—or ourselves as time would prove.

We still had a long journey back to the city of Oradea where the Church was waiting for us. When we came to a phone, a call was placed to pastor Negrutz telling him we were in Romania but more than a day's travel away. He was elated and said that the church was packed with standing room only. Thousands were praying for us. So, we set our face toward the north and through ice and snow made our way slowly back. Everywhere we went we felt that the police were watching us or looking for us. It was unnerving.

Through the Baptistry

The next afternoon we arrived at our destination in Oradea, Romania. Our van pulled up to the church house. We could not believe the size of the crowd as hundreds were standing outside trying to get in. The powerful singing could be heard outside when we stepped out of the van. Because the aisles were jammed with standing room only; the question became, "how do we get me, the preacher, to the pulpit area?" Someone had already thought that out. As Sam and Jon were led elsewhere, I was led to a side

145

door. The small hallway took us to an area directly behind the stage and pulpit. A man took my big coat and gloves then said, *"Follow me"*. He opened a small door and I looked in. I was looking at the Baptistry—empty of water, but a large tub none the less. Because the man leading me spoke little or no English he just pointed for me to step into the empty tub! I did, and he then opened a curtain. There I stood looking out over a huge mass of people! A roar of excitement went up from the crowd as they saw me standing in their baptistry. Quickly some of those on stage, including Pastor Paul Negrutz, helped me climb out and onto the stage. What an entrance! I have had some pretty exciting and sometimes unusual preaching experiences, but that was one destiny moment to remember. Wow!

Risk and Reward

I am telling you this story for your encouragement. There are times when fulfilling your Destiny will require you to believe what others cannot believe or to go where others fear to go—and have faith! There is a risk and a reach that goes with the destiny territory. I have learned over my years of following Christ that God never leads you where He cannot follow or where He cannot provide for your safety and success. I remember when I sat down next to Paul Negrutz on the church stage, in the midst of the singing; he leaned over to my ear and said, *"See those two men in suits sitting on the front row of the choir loft. They are not choir singers, they are police. Someone must have told them you were coming."* Oh boy, here we go! That night I preached the gospel to the secret police. That wasn't the last we were to see of them. Those guys followed us everywhere we went for an entire week. When finally it was time for us to leave Romania and return to Budapest, Hungary, the police were waiting for us at the border.

A long cold Harassment

Arriving at the border just after 2pm on this very frigid January day; we no sooner stepped out of the van at the checkpoint, than the Immigration Police began to interrogate us one by one. They took Jon first, maybe being the youngest they thought they could break him down for information. Sam and I had prepped each other about what might happen so we were prepared for the drill. Well, not totally! It got very intense the next 25 hours.

First Jon, then Sam, then I were questioned about whom we knew, met and visited while in Romania. The waiting room was not heated so we had to keep walking around to keep warm. Jon was wearing Texas cowboy boots and his feet nearly froze. As each man was taken away by the police at the barrel end of an AK-47, the remaining two of us determined to just be God's men in God's place at God's time. We told them why we were in Romania (of course they knew already as we had been preaching in several churches!) Each of us was stripped down to our underwear at gunpoint, then questioned for hours. All except me; my turn came last. It seems they figured I was the leader since I was preaching in the Oradea church. Not true, Sam Friend was the leader, but they questioned me last. It was after midnight when a top immigration or police official arrived. He was all dressed up in his big Army coat, hat and uniform, very imposing. By this time we were cold, exhausted, and somewhat frightened by their repeated threats to put us in jail unless we told them what they wanted. When the guards and the big man came for me, I jokingly told Sam and Jon to wait for me, I'd be right back!

By my Side

I have memorized scripture since I was a teenager. As I walked into the interrogation room and was told to strip at gunpoint, the police official began to tell me he had traveled all the way from Bucharest to question me. He said we were in big trouble. He again threatened jail time for us. I immediately thought of Acts 2:25, spoken by Peter at Pentecost, *"I saw the Lord always before me. Because He is at my right hand, I will not be shaken."* At that moment God's boldness came over me like a mighty force. I interrupted the guy, and said, *"Listen, I can save us all a lot of time. I don't know what you think we have done or what laws you think we have broken, but we have done nothing illegal. We entered your country with valid passports, and since being here have preached the gospel of Jesus Christ openly in your churches. Furthermore, do you know who we are?"* He said he knew the names on our passports only. I challenged him again, *"I think you have a file on us. Sam Friend and I have been coming to your country for several years now. You turned us away from the border two weeks ago. I think you are angry that we were allowed to enter Romania without your permission. So, you and I need to come to an understanding. Before leaving the American Embassy in Budapest last week, a phone call was placed to David Funderburk, the US Ambassador to Romania. He is expecting us to call him tomorrow from the American Embassy in Budapest. If Ambassador Funderburk does not hear from us by noon tomorrow, he will come looking for us! You my friend need to know that we are important American preachers with friends in the United States Senate and Congress. So go ahead and put us in jail. You will make us famous, but I promise you this—you will lose your job and be embarrassed that you treated God's servants so disrespectfully. If you are fond of those Epaulets on your shoulder, you need to release us* and *send us on our way."* Soon as those bold words came out of my mouth I sat there (in my underwear) fearful of what the Capitan would do.

Free to Go

The man sat there stunned, almost speechless. As I saw an opening, I just continued to tell him that Jesus loved him and I loved him too! I said all this while sitting on a cold metal chair nearly naked! He was not very receptive but he was sizing up the situation. It was clear to me that he believed what I told him about Ambassador Funderburk. Before I could say another word, he stormed out of the room. Only a few minutes later I was told by a young guard to get dressed and he took me back to Sam and Jon in the lobby. Sam and Jon were curious why my interview was so short. I said, *"Guys, we are either going to prison, or we are leaving Romania very soon."* Almost immediately we were given our passports and other items and told to leave. It happened so fast we were totally unprepared for our release. The Spirit of God had somehow convinced the "big man" that he had made a mistake in detaining us. I remember looking at my watch—it was 3 o'clock in the morning. We had been there at that checkpoint over 24 hours!

What do we do now?

As we climbed into our van, which had been thoroughly searched by the border patrol, we saw what a mess they had made of our luggage and other belongings. I guess they thought they would catch us smuggling drugs, Bibles, or I don't know what. Soon as we started the cold engine, Sam said, *"We have no petrol. I had planned to buy a full tank in Hungary where it is cheaper. We cannot go far on an empty tank at three o'clock in the morning."* I replied, *"Not only that, look across the fence at the Hungarian border guards. Those guys have been watching this van for a day and a night. They probably think we are smugglers or worse."* That's when we fervently and thankfully prayed. Each of us, sitting there in that chilling air, began to thank God for His watch care and deliverance. He had not forsaken us so we trusted Him to get us through the next border crossing into Communist Hungary! We asked for the Father's continued favor upon us. Somehow we would survive this.

A modern day Miracle

It was a strange experience driving that one hundred or so yards across "no man's land' to the Hungarian border. We just knew our van lights going before us were leading us to impending danger. It was very quiet in the car as the three of us pulled up to the gate. A soldier opened the gate looking intently at us. I wonder why! We slowly got out of the van at the checkpoint. Expecting frowns and hostility from the Hungarian border officials we were amazed when the young soldier greeted us with a smile and welcomed us into the lobby. What was that smile all about? Was this a wolf licking his chops?

As you might expect, we were the only customers at 3AM. Without delay of any kind, we were escorted to the immigration desk and one man began to process our passports. He too greeted us with a smile and began to curiously ask us why the Romanians had kept us so long and had searched our vehicle so thoroughly. Sam, Jon, and I just told him the truth. The man spoke no English and we spoke no Hungarian; so Sam and I tried to communicate in German. Great, the man spoke some German. Brokenly, I

DESTINY: YOU AND GOD

struggled to tell him we were all Baptist preachers. Why I said "Baptist" preacher I do not know except that was the key word. The official excitedly said to us in German, "Ich bin eine baptiste!" (I am a Baptist) Sam and I looked at each other in amazement. Are you kidding me? At that time less than one percent of the populations of Hungary were Baptists. What are the odds? Encouraged, I told him we were friends of a Baptist pastor in Budapest and I named Pastor Geza Kovacs. The man's eyes lit up as he exclaimed joyfully, "Meine Pastor ist Geza Kovacs"(Geza Kovacs is my pastor). I said, "Yes Gaza pastors the BudaFok Baptist church in Budapest." Again this official delightedly said, "BudaFok ist meiner kirche!"(My church is Buda Folk). At this point we three sojourners in a strange land are wondering—who is this guy, is he for real or is he surreal?

Petrol down the Road

Now we are no longer strangers but rather brothers in need of help. The Hungarian communist official, who just happened to be a Baptist and a member of the only church in Hungary I had ever been in, now got to work to assist us on our way. When he was told we had no petrol, he got on the phone and got somebody out of bed, telling them to turn their lights on at their petrol station because we were coming their way in a few minutes. We had no Hungarian money, but the Baptist brother said to get what we needed to get on down the road and he would pay the petrol guy later. We thanked the man profusely "danke, danke" and started up the van with the official and soldiers waving us goodbye! Really! As we drove off, looking for the petrol station with lights on at 4AM; I said to the guys, *"What just happened back there? Was that a Hungarian angel God sent to deliver us?"* Maybe it was three angels, one for each of us. We were dumbfounded by it all. We got the gas tank filled and headed down the highway to Budapest. Later, in Budapest, when we met with Pastor Geza Kovacs, he had no idea who the immigration official was. He further said one has to be a member of the Communist party to get a job like that. Now we know there are no Baptist communists –right? Anyway,

150

DESTINY: YOU AND GOD

there you have it. Living dangerously in the center of God's will—fulfilling destiny, watching God the Father do His thing!

DESTINY POINTERS:

1. There really is a "risk and reward" paradigm in God's Kingdom. When a young man like Daniel refuses to worship an idol (the King) then God shows up with an Angel in the fiery furnace. Has that ever happened to you, when God rewarded your risk taking with angelic power and presence? I hope so!
2. When we are living out destiny through obedience to God's call; we are invincible and indestructible until He is finished with us. Do you believe that? You must believe it, or you'll never live a destiny filled life.
3. Moments of destiny require an unyielding faith. However, an unyielding faith can sometimes be your downfall if:
    a) your motives are not pure,
    b) your pride steps in the way, or
    c) your arrogance squelches God's voice.

How do you know when this happens and how do you balance this with destiny determination?

Chapter Seventeen

Destiny and the Call of God

God's call is greater than all our regrets and failures.

Today I visited a place called the Holy Spirit Hospital (HSH) in Dallas, Texas where I live. My friend Smokey John Reeves operates a Bar-B-Q restaurant that every Tuesday becomes the HSH during the noon hour. Folks from all strata of Dallas society come there for lunch and spiritual nourishment as well. The Holy Spirit shows up—a lot!

Smokey told a group of about 50 of a recent experience he had when asked to speak to the graduating class of Dallas Theological Seminary. Being led of God's Spirit, Smokey's topic was, "If God didn't call you—quit!"

He said that after the meeting was adjourned, 25 graduates went back to his restaurant to talk to him for two hours. Several who were preparing to pastor churches were seriously questioning whether God had really called them. Their training in Hebrew and Greek was no substitute for a calling. What is strange about this is that Smokey John is a business man with no theological education whatsoever. However, he mentors, disciples, preaches, and often blesses many people with his faith, compassion, and wisdom. People are attracted to Smokey not because he is smart

DESTINY: YOU AND GOD

or educated, but because they see and feel the call of God on his life. That call points to destiny; it is evidential of God's purpose being fulfilled in Smokey's life.

The Call to Destiny

Our 21st Century world view doesn't embrace or believe much in what the Bible describes as "God's call." Yet so much of the Bible's message is about that very thing.

"To those who are called according to His purpose." Romans 8:28

"And whom He predestined, these He also called; and whom He called He also justified..."Romans 8:30

"God is faithful, through whom you were called into fellowship with His Son, Jesus Christ our Lord." 1st Corinthians 1:9

"I am amazed that you are so quickly deserting Him who called you by the grace of Christ..." Galatians 1:6

"The gifts and callings of God are irrevocable" Romans 11:29

These mysterious yet wonderful verses are telling us that God has his radar gun on us. We are in His sights. His heart is toward us, for us, and is calling us to Himself. This "call" of God is destiny's voice in our ear. He is calling us upward to our predestined potential. How you respond to His call shapes your future, even your eternity. So many of our wails of despair have come from our missing of God's call. The sense of loss can be unbearable.

God's Call and Regrets

Mark Batterson notes research done by two psychologists from Cornell University which found that passing time is a vital element in actions we regret verses inaction regrets. The research showed that in a week 57% regretted wrong actions taken and 43% regretted inactions of things not done that should have been done. However, when quizzed about action regrets verses inaction regrets over the course of one's life, the divergence was remarkably reversed. A disproportionate 84% said they greatly felt the loss of

DESTINY: YOU AND GOD

"inaction regrets" verses only 14% who had strong regrets over "action regrets."[1] This clearly tells us some things we need to know about ourselves. We can get over and get past sins committed; we can even be forgiven of them and move on. Yet, over the course of one's life, we cannot so easily forgive ourselves for those actions we did not take, those dreams we dared not pursue, or those visions we left unfulfilled. To have lived your life and look back and see that you failed to really live your life will be your greatest regret. A missionary friend of mine sent me these words about regret:

Beware lest we come to the end of our days looking back:

Regretting sinful patterns of behavior that never got confronted and changed.
Or abilities and gifts that never got cultivated and deployed.
Of deep intimate gut-wrenchingly honest conversations you never had;
of exhilarating risks you never took,
sacrificial gifts you never offered,
great bold prayers you never prayed,
and lives you never touched.
Until weeks become months,
and months turn into years,
and one day you're looking back on your life
as you're sitting in a recliner with a shriveled soul;
with forgotten, unfulfilled dreams.
And you realize there was a world of desperate need,
and a great God calling you to be part of something bigger than yourself —
You see the person you could have become but did not.
You never followed your calling.
You never dared to run the race, or to win the prize.
You failed yourself, your God and your destiny.
God Forbid! O' My God!

Over the years so many men have expressed regret that their moment of destiny passed them by. They do not say it in destiny language, but that is what they mean. Recently a businessman friend surprised me with the news that when he was a youth, he definitely felt God's call on his life to be a missionary. He told his dad of his desire only to be met with strong opposition. His father told him missionaries die poor, have no family ties, and that he should pursue the family business. He followed his father's advice and went to a university majoring in business and finance. He pleased his father by entering the family business, making money, and in the process lost his dream and passion. In hindsight, he pleased the wrong father. His heavenly Father's plan got placed on the back burner. Eternity served the temporal at great loss to many. Has this happened to you?

Maybe you had a destiny moment when God clearly called you to join His team and you missed it through rebellion, neglect, fear or faithlessness. It is a sad thing to have regrets over opportunities missed, but it is tragic to miss a life calling. I am reminded again of Paul's words in Roman 11:29 *"for the gifts and the calling of God are irrevocable."* He was speaking of Israel as God's people of choice. Intriguing is the destiny idea of God's "calling" on a man. Paul says that calling is irrevocable. Let me explain. When God calls you—to salvation, to service, to a particular mission or task, you need to say "yes" and obey immediately. Why, because God's call on your life is your destiny marker. It is not an option for you, it IS you. His call is that which should define who you are. If you refuse, resist or rebel, that does not change God's mind, will or purpose for you. It only means you are off the track heading for a train wreck!

Aaron Burr

Those familiar with American history know the name Aaron Burr. He was one of those very bright stars that shown in the night sky of the early American dream. Aaron Burr Jr. was the only son of Aaron Burr Sr., a Presbyterian pastor and first President of what is now Princeton University. Aaron Burr's mother was the daughter of the distinguished minister Jonathan Edwards. Sadly at age three Aaron lost both parents. Within months of each other,

DESTINY: YOU AND GOD

his father and mother died; as did his grandfather. He and his sister were raised by his uncle Timothy Edwards. His upbringing was evangelical Calvinism. He even went to Princeton at age 13 to study religion in the footsteps of his famous father and grandfather.

A Destiny Turning Point

Remarkably, young Aaron Burr graduated from Princeton at age seventeen in 1772. There is a story that comes out of Aaron's college days that is very revealing and foreboding of his future destiny. These were the days of the Great Awakening and the Princeton campus was profoundly stirred by a mighty movement of God's Spirit. Young Burr was moved by the spiritual revival on the campus; so much so that he went to seek counsel from John Witherspoon, the university President.[2] Aaron asked Dr. Witherspoon if he should join the awakening and commit his life to serving Christ, maybe even become a minister like his father and grandfather. Dr. Witherspoon urged him to calm down; and to let all this religious excitement pass, then make up his mind later. What followed were months of torment and conviction. Burr was resisting God's call on his life. In the autumn of the next year Aaron Burr came to live with Dr. Joseph Bellamy, of Bethlehem, Connecticut. Dr.Bellamy was a famous theologian and spiritual leader of the Great Awakening. Obviously, young Burr was conflicted about following Christ. The delays were deadly to Aaron Burr's faith. Over time he deliberately rejected the gospel and adopted the infidelity then so rife in Europe and America. Burr became an intellectual follower of Lord Chesterfield of England, never to return to faith in Christ again.

We know most of Aaron Burr's turbulent story. He turned from grace to law and rather than become a preacher, he became a politician. In 1800 at age 44, he ran for U.S. President against Thomas Jefferson only to be defeated by the narrowest of margins—one electoral vote. He became the third Vice President in U.S. history. In 1804 he killed his friend turned rival Alexander Hamilton in a gun duel. Thus began his decline. Although history

157

is not clear on his motives, it seems Aaron Burr tried to set himself up as Emperor over what is now Texas, Louisiana and much of Mexico. He was tried for treason, and although acquitted, his career and reputation were forever ruined. For several years he lived in exile in Europe and became penniless, struggling the remainder of his life to find meaning and significance.

However, there is a piece of the story often not told. It is reported that in his later years, while living a quiet life in New York City, Aaron Burr was walking down a street one evening when he heard hymn singing coming from a nearby church. Curious, he walked up to the door and stood outside listening. A Christian man, maybe a member of the church, came up to him and asked Mr. Burr if he was a Christian. Aaron looked at the man and said, *"Strange that you should ask me that question—sir, my name is Aaron Burr"*. Then he told the Christian witness the story of his days of spiritual awakening at Princeton those many years ago. He told how the Spirit of God had called him to faith in Christ, but he had refused. Aaron Burr then said these telling words, *"I said no to Christ those many years ago, and he has never been back to me in quite the same way since."* A moment in time, a calling, a rejection, destiny lost and a wasted, ruined life. Now in old age he has only regrets. On his death bed Aaron Burr is said to have affirmed his belief that the Holy Scriptures are *"the most perfect system of truth the world has ever seen."* [3]

It makes you wonder what Aaron Burr's life could have been had he said "yes" instead of "no." What kind of impact could this very brilliant, charismatic leader had had on the world. We will never know. We can only share his regrets.

When God calls, we had better listen and obey. Has he spoken to you recently? Did you heed the Spirit or quench the Spirit? A failed life and missed destiny is made up of those micro moments of God's callings often rejected. When repeatedly quenched—the fire dies out.

Failure and Regret

To fail or miss God's call can be fatal; but it need not be final.

DESTINY: YOU AND GOD

Failure is the product of both actions taken that we should not have taken or it is the result of being inactive, refusing to take the action steps we should have taken. Regret is the trailing emotion to those actions or inactions. Listen carefully—our God is bigger than your failures. Missing God's call yesterday does not disqualify you from today's destiny call. Our paralyzing regrets can cause us to never believe again. Faith in God's mercy and purpose will drive away regrets over failed callings in the past. In Christ our yesterdays are a cancelled check; our tomorrows a promissory note, but our todays are God's money in hand. His grace generates his call to us to believe him and begin again. Paul was absolutely right on the mark, *"The gifts and callings of God are irrevocable."*

Grace that is Greater…

Over fifty years ago I was a student in a small Christian University studying for the Gospel ministry. While there I met an Oklahoma cowboy, who had been on the rodeo circuit. He had married his high school sweetheart and they competed in rodeos together; she a barrel racer, he a bronco rider. They had a son and all seemed to be going well for this cowboy couple. Then came the Call of God. My cowboy friend was saved and called to preach simultaneously. His young bride did not like it or accept it. She had married a cowboy—not a preacher. She left him to pursue her rodeo career. When I met him, he was trying to go to school and raise his little boy at the same time. Sadly my friend learned that being a divorced preacher in Oklahoma's Bible belt was a death sentence to his calling and hopes of ever being a preacher. Yet he knew God had called him so he trusted in God and did the best he could. He later married the girl who is with him today after fifty years of marriage. They have become some of God's choicest servants these many years, but not without moving past their failures and regrets.

They never were allowed to pastor in the south, but God needed them in the Northwestern United States. So as kids out of seminary they ventured to the Great Northwest and began a small church in Washington. After some twenty five years, they together built a mighty mission minded church in the Seattle area. I look at what

DESTINY: YOU AND GOD

God has done through them and it reminds me that God's callings are not only irrevocable, but they are flexible! My word to you is, never quit on God because He will never quit on you.

When things go wrong, as they sometimes will,
When the road your on seems all up hill,
When the funds are low and the debts are high,
And you want to smile, but you have to cry,
When care is pressing you down a bit,
Rest if you must, but don't you quit.

Life is queer with its twists and turns,
as every one of us sometimes learns.
And many a fellow turns about,
When he might have won had he stuck it out.
Don't give up though the pace seems slow,
You might succeed with another blow.

Often the goal is nearer than...
It seems to a faint and faltering man;
Often the struggler has given up,
When he might have captured the coveted cup;
And he learned too late when night came down,
How close he was to the golden crown.

Success is failure turned inside out
The silver tint of the cloud of doubt,
And you never can tell how close you are
It may be near when it seems so far.
So stick to the fight when you are hardest hit...
It's when things seem worst that you mustn't quit.
Author Unknown

Like Simon Peter of old, we may fail Christ, but it will not deter His destiny plans for us. He saw your failure as part and parcel to His plan. Your faith in God's mercy and loving kindness

DESTINY: YOU AND GOD

will overcome failure and regret. What He called you to in the past, may not even be similar to what He has purposed for you today. This drama of life we are in is not a Kodak moment; it is a streaming video being filmed as we live it. Someone once said, "the faith that falters before the finish was faulty from the first.' A clever saying, but not true as it relates to our destiny. A better saying is found in Romans, "*If God is for us — who can be against us?*"[4] Paul then proceeds to list the multiple things that you would think might hinder God's purpose in us. He says that life, death, angels, struggles, wars, tragedies, persecutions, famines or whatever else Satan himself can throw at us—none of them can separate us from God's unfailing love for us. He will do His part if we will do ours. You might ask what great thing we must do to overcome failure, sin, and regret. Simply say you are sorry and mean it. That is right—that is all it takes to begin again with our Father/God. *"If we confess our sins He is faithful and just to forgive us our sins and cleanse us of all unrighteousness.*[5] Meaning that even today, in this moment God is calling us to destiny—are you listening? Will you report for duty?

The Olympic Creed

In 1908 Pierre de Coubertin got the idea for this phrase from a speech given by Bishop Ethelbert Talbot at a service for Olympic champions during the 1908 Olympic Games. The Olympic Creed reads: *"The most important thing in the Olympic Games is not to win but to take part, just as the most important thing in life is not the triumph but the struggle. The essential thing is not to have conquered but to have fought well."*

DESTINY POINTERS:

1. Have you responded in faith to God's call to salvation in Jesus Christ? He calls you—you must call him back, "whosoever will call upon the name of the Lord will be saved."Romans 10:13
2. When was the last time you consciously heard God's call? What was He calling you to do? Or was He calling you to "be."?
3. How have you dealt with the failures in your life; a close

161

examination would be good for you. Do you live your life in the reality that God does not grade on the curve? Because we are forgiven in Christ we must forgive ourselves. Have you done that?

4. What things have you regretted that you did not do? Were these seeded in God's purpose for you? Is there still time and is God calling you to now follow this nudge? How will you respond?

CHAPTER EIGHTEEN

Your Destiny as God's Mosaic

I've really screwed up my life; I'm destined to fail—really?

So often we meet those poor souls who have been beaten up by life and have quit on any idea of a God fulfilling destiny. They have buried significance and married survival. It is to those eaten up with failure or bound by boredom that I write this encouragement. We really need to see our failures as God the Father sees them, not as our culture sees them. Our perception is seldom God's reality.

Destiny's Heroes

It really helps me to cope with my failures and losses by taking a careful look at how God has told His story and who His main actors really are. By now I hope you are convinced that the Bible is God's destiny story; in fact, some say that the "Bible" stands for *Basic Instructions Before Leaving Earth!* He tells His story using imperfect saints in the drama. Without exception, they all are flawed. Let me tell you the story of Jacob. If you are not familiar with him, Jacob is prototypical of a man being carried along by Destiny. It took him years to get there but God did not quit on Jacob until Jacob was clay molded in the Master's hands. In fulfilling destiny, the breaking usually precedes the blessing; this was surely true in Jacob's journey with God. It will probably be true in yours.

The Cheater

Those familiar with the Genesis account of Jacob's life know he started out with an ugly nickname. Jacob in Hebrew is loosely translated, "He who clutches the heel." Jacob (a twin) was second born, coming out of Rebecca's womb holding his brother's (Esau) heel. His nickname became "cheater." Now how's that for a start in life? And, as often happens, the name became a self-fulfilling prophecy. Jacob's story is profound because it shows us how vividly God operates in and through sinful human beings. If God can shape history through a man like Jacob, then there is much hope for the rest of us!

Being the first born son of Isaac, Esau is his daddy's favorite. He is a real man's man, while Jacob is a mama's boy. Rebecca covets that Jacob should have Esau's birthright and Isaac's blessing. With mama's help Jacob, the cheater, steals both favored positions from Esau. The rest of Jacob's story is taken up with Jacob running from Esau and running from God. However, God is the God of Abraham, Isaac, and Jacob. The *"and Jacob"* part is the destiny part of Jacob's life. God comes looking for Jacob to lead him into His pre-destined purpose for Jacobs's life.

New Name New Destiny

Jacob meets God one night while sleeping beside a creek.[1] A mighty angel seeks a destiny encounter with Jacob. A wrestling match takes place the outcome of which changes Jacob forever. The angel strikes Jacob's thigh and as a result he will limp the rest of his life as a reminder of this destiny moment. He also is given a God-name to replace the nick-name. The angel names him Israel, and he will father a great nation after his new name.

So, what can we learn from this remarkable story? There are many lessons, but the one central truth is that God can begin with us at any point in our story. Your past does not determine your future. Failure is never final and seldom fatal; not when God has a plan for you. Our history can be tainted like Jacobs but God can change your heart, your history, and even your name. What you used to be "known for" can be erased in a destiny encounter with Christ whose purposes are eternally bigger than our frayed and failing lives.

Mosaics

I was sitting in a beautiful cathedral in Lintz, Austria a few years ago looking intently at the fantastic art work in the windows. While sitting there I had this thought that my life is like that glass Mosaic. It is made up of broken pieces of glass that some master artist put together in such a way that the brokenness has turned into beauty. The mosaic is not made from perfect pieces but from fallen, broken pieces. A beautiful mosaic picture is made up of many pieces of glass—different textures, colors and sizes. When the pieces are separate lying randomly on the table, they do not look like much, just worthless broken pieces of glass. Our lives are like that until God's destiny lays hold of us. In His hands we can be a part of the Master Designer's mosaic of history. When by faith we chose to be the broken pieces He can use, He then turns broken pieces of glass into designer pieces of grace. Put together by the master artist they become a visual message profound and beautiful, full of meaning and purpose. Each piece is a part of the whole to make the Mosaic message complete. When redeemed we become pieces of His destined purpose—destined to be glorious! Wow! Is that beautiful or what?

I found a song by Shelley Johnson that says it so very well:

> *Just a pile of broken glass*
> *Pieces of a painful past*
> *Shattered by the storms of life*
> *This is all that's left inside*
>
> *He can take the fallen pieces*
> *And lay them in the perfect place*
> *And when His work is finally finished*
> *You will be a mosaic of grace.*

DESTINY: YOU AND GOD

In your pain you may not see
The beauty of the Masterpiece
But there's a greater work of art
Than what each piece alone imparts
Hallelujah hallelu, to the God who makes all things new
Hallelujah hallelu hallelu
He will take the fallen pieces
And lay them in the perfect place
And when His work is finally finished
You are a Mosaic of grace! [2]

Breaking, Broken, Blessed

Have you ever noticed that we become stronger in the broken places? Doctors tell us that bones are often stronger where broken, then healed. People are like that too. Those destiny shapers and destiny makers that God uses are often just like Jacob. What he was—is not who he became. God uses the breaking in order to bring us to the end of ourselves, and then all we want or have left is Him and His will for us. Those are the folks God can make into a Mosaic through which He can bless others.

DESTINY POINTERS:

1. Have you allowed guilt, shame or failures to keep you from pursuing your potential?
2. Are you willing to begin again by believing in the God who never stops loving you?
3. There is a healing place, a forgiveness place and a place of beginning again. That place is the Cross of Christ. Have you made the journey there recently?
4. Are you willing to give God your broken pieces and let Him make designer pieces of them? When you are willing, He is able. Destiny awaits you. In fact, it is made of those broken pieces. Somebody needs what God just taught you through your brokenness.

Chapter Nineteen

Destiny and the Terminal Generation

The King is coming; will we live to see the last act of the drama?

Frances Schaeffer, one of the foremost Christian thinkers of the 20th century, wrote a very prophetic book in the 1970's titled *How Should We Then Live: The Rise and Fall of Western Thought and Culture*. Dr. Schaeffer's message was predictive of the total decline of Christian culture in the western world. He followed that book with another entitled, *The Church at the End of the Twentieth Century*, in which he predicted that by the beginning of the 21st century western civilization would be in "the post-Christian" era. Both books were very influential to the thinking of thousands, me included. He got me to thinking seriously about living my life as though my generation might be the last generation before Christ's return.

Even a decade or so before that, while I was a university freshman, my heart was beginning to feel a destiny bent. I was enrolled in a small Christian university preparing myself for the ministry. One beautiful spring day I was sitting in a New Testament class when the professor brought up the subject of the Jews and their rejection of Jesus as the Messiah. I had begun preaching while in high school, and was well on my way to becoming an evangelist, following in the footsteps of Billy Graham (my hero).

The Bible I used for preaching at that young age was a Scofield Reference Bible. In my zeal as a youth I thought the printed notes in the Scofield bible were as inspired as the rest of the text! I was a zealot of the first order. Already at that young age I was excited about the possibility of Christ's return in my lifetime. I had been influenced by the notes in the Scofield bible telling me the Jews would one day be restored to their Homeland. My professor saw no significance in Israel as part of God's plan for the future.

Do you know how many Arabs there are?

During those years of the late 1950's, it was only a few years before (1948) that Israel had become a nation again in Palestine. So I eagerly raised my hand in class to ask a question of the professor. I said, "Sir, since the Jews have returned to the holy land, and since Jerusalem is divided off between Jews and Palestinians, do you think the prophecies will come true and Israel will take back the Temple mount and reclaim Jerusalem?" [1] The professor smiled a condescending smile and replied," Young man any attempt by the Israelis to take back the Temple Mount would cause an Arab-Israeli war." I impulsively said, "Well, doesn't the Bible prophesy that the Jews will win and take back the land God promised to them? Isaiah and Ezekiel say they will return and rebuild the Temple before Christ returns." Now I was really asking for it. The "it" being humiliation! The wise professor said, "Son. Do you know how many Jews there are today in Israel?" I meekly said about two million. "Correct you are, and do you know how many Muslim Arabs there are in the area?" I shook my head horizontally. "Well, son there are twenty million; and they will not give up the Holy sites without first trying to destroy Israel." So, that was the end of that class discussion. My tail between my freshman legs, I retreated.

Nine years later

I graduated from the university with a Bible major and headed off to Seminary. During this period of schooling and biblical studies I became more and more convinced that God had done something prophetic in restoring Israel as a nation. It seemed to me only a matter of time until the Jews came all the way home. During the 1960's tensions mounted between Israel, Syria, Egypt and Jordan. In early June of 1967, Israel attacked Egypt and all the Middle East exploded into war. Fighting against incredible odds and outnumbered twenty to one, Israel in six days of intense but strategic fighting won the day. As the Israeli army marched into old Jerusalem they came to the ancient wall of the temple. There the Israeli commander Moshe Dayan, declared to the news cameras, "We are home, never to leave again!" I remember that moment well. It was a validation to me of destiny fulfilled. From that moment on, I have had a very strong sense of destiny. That event confirmed anew my belief in the prophetic scriptures. I could really believe that we might live to see the end as the terminal generation. By "terminal generation" I mean there is coming (if not already here) a generation whose destiny it is to be the last generation on earth. Those living when Christ returns to establish the Kingdom are indeed the last (terminal) generation.

Destiny as Terminus

So now I want you to think on destiny not just as your God ordained journey here on earth, but to also think of it as destination, the end of the journey. Looking at God's Big Story—this biblical meta-narrative has a dramatic ending. The prayer of Christ, *"thy kingdom come, thy will be done on earth as it is in heaven,'* is going to be answered—and very soon. The Bible's big picture story climaxes with Christ predicted return to earth as King of Kings. He returns to fulfill destiny. All that was lost in Eden with man's rebellion will be restored when the King returns to establish His Kingdom on Earth. So, when we think of our destiny being fulfilled, I like to think of it in three phases:

Our destiny is our life journey and purpose—our part in the Drama God is directing.

Our destiny is also our destination—our final rest from the journey—heaven.

DESTINY: YOU AND GOD

Our destiny could be as the terminal generation—seeing Christ's return.

None of us knows who that terminal generation will be; but scripture warns us to be watchful and ready for Christ's return. There are many of us who see strong indicators on the horizon of a gathering storm. Serious Bible students see a unique destiny for those living in these days of the early 21st century.

Destiny Events

Let me explain my thinking on this subject. Jesus in his message to his disciples on the Mount of Olives just prior to his death has enormous importance to us today. It is recorded in Matthew 24 and gives us some very specific clues to destiny events that must take place before His return. Let me list them for you:

1. **The re-establishment of the Nation Israel**—Jesus predicted in Matthew 24:32 that the *"fig tree would blossom when summer is near."* His reference to the blooming fig tree is an allusion to the restoration of the Jews to their ancient homeland. This prophecy had partial fulfillment in 1948 and again in 1967. To many scholars, the terminal generation began with Israel's victory in the Six day war in June 1967. Whether this is the beginning or not, it certainly is a destiny marker in history for Christ's return. You and I have lived to see it happen. When the Jews came home—the angels began dusting off the trumpets and saddling up the horses.

2. **Rebuilding the Temple in Jerusalem**—Jesus predicted that among those returning Jews would be a zealous group who will push hard to rebuild the temple and re-establish ancient sacrifices. Matthew 24:15 tells us the Antichrist will *"stand in the Holy place."* 2nd Thessalonians 2:4 says Antichrist will *"oppose and exalt himself above all that is called god or object of worship, so that he takes his seat in the temple of God, displaying himself as being* God." Logic would say that the Temple must be built before Antichrist can set up his headquarters there. Already the plans have been drawn and

readiness made for the quick construction of a marvelous new Temple. That day is on the horizon. We could be that generation that sees this wondrous prophetic event.

3. The Great Apostasy—Matthew 24:11-13 and 2nd Thessalonians 2:3 describe a "great falling away" from the Christian faith just before Christ's return. This is caused by many factors not least of all is the world–wide persecution of the church which reaches its zenith in the rise of the Antichrist.

4. World-wide Evangelism—In Matthew 24:14, Jesus tells us He will not return until all the nations hear the Gospel message of salvation. We stand on the threshold of history being fulfilled in this prophecy. We are the generation that has the will, the power and the technology to tell every nation of God's love in Jesus Christ. The generation that fulfills this destiny will see Christ's return. There is coming a day in history when the last person God purposes to save—will be saved. *"Then comes the end,"* Jesus said.

5. The coming of Antichrist—Jesus in Matthew 24:15-22 predicts that Messiah's return will be preceded by the coming of a world dictator who is the embodiment of Evil. Scripture calls him by many names—all of them bad! He is the abomination of desolation, the great dragon, the Beast, the Man of sin, and the Antichrist. Jesus, Paul and John predict his rise to power just prior to Christ's return.

When Worlds Collide

You and I can sense that some of these events are taking place now and some are possible in the near future. It seems that cultures that were once oceans apart are now on a collision course. There is now so much talk of "one world" that such talk seems common place. One economy, one world government, one common currency, and one world leader is the repeated mantra. The common rhetoric is that we are moving from many nations to "United Nations." These gathering storm clouds are moving us toward a destiny that will test the people of God. The Church will be tested in the fires of persecution and sifted like wheat to remove the true from the false, the good from the bad. Scholars see in Daniel's prophecy a coming seven year reign of Antichrist. [2] The Revelation also describes this seven year tribulation of the beast. Bible students call it The Great Tribulation. It is popular teaching among many evangelical Christians that Christ will return to "rapture" His church away before the reign of Antichrist. This teaching would have all Christ followers escape suffering and martyrdom at the hands of Antichrist. If they are raptured, they are also rescued. While there is much scriptural teaching that true Christ followers will escape the wrath of God that comes down on Antichrist and those who worship him; there is no guarantee we will be rescued from the wrath of Antichrist.

Raptured: Yes—but when?

There is much evidence in scripture that the rapture will not precede the wrath of Antichrist and that both the Church and Jews will suffer his initial wrath. Should this be true (and I think it is) then it means some near future generation of Christ followers will be destined to have it "tuff." [3]

An explanation might be needed here. Millions of evangelical Christians believe in a sudden, any moment "taking up" of the true church before the rise of Antichrist and his persecution. Also there are many Bible students who expect Christ to "rapture" His church, but do not see a pre-tribulation time line in the scriptures. We see the distinct possibility that the church will suffer at the hand of this Satan inspired world leader called Antichrist. We see a generation of Christ followers who will suffer and even inspire a generation of Jews and Israelis to follow Christ as their Messiah. The issue is the *when* of Christ's return to take His bride away, not the fact that He will do so. Just move the date back 42 months and you have a generation of Christ follower's at great risk.[4]

Destiny's Martyrs

Those Christ followers who live to see Antichrist will have a unique destiny. It is their lot to suffer and even die for their faith in

Christ as no other generation has ever suffered. This testing is both their agony and their glory. The book of Revelation describes them as those saints whose destiny it is to reject the worship of Antichrist (the "beast") and refuse the mark of the beast (666). That generation of believers will suffer the loss of all things material for Christ's sake. They cannot buy or sell without the mark of the beast. To refuse to worship the beast will seal their death. Thousands upon thousands will die a martyr's death. They are destined for glory as well. Revelation says of them, *"Here is the perseverance of the saints who keep the commandments of God and their faith in Jesus. And I heard a voice from heaven, saying, 'Write, Blessed are the dead who die in the Lord from now on!' 'Yes, says the Spirit, 'that they may rest from their labors, for their deeds follow with them.'"* [5] Revelation also proclaims the martyr's victory, *"and they overcame him* (antichrist) *because of the blood of the Lamb and because of the word of their testimony, and they did not love their life even unto death."*[6] Notice they die, but they also overcome. How can this be? It is so because Christ is coming immediately afterward to raise those faithful martyrs from the grave. They will reign with Him in His kingdom. They are destined not only to die a martyr's death, but also destined to wear a martyr's crown. That terminal generation has the privilege of seeing "Kingdom come," that Jesus told us to expect.

Just Suppose

My thinking is that living today there are millions of Christ followers who are that terminal generation. We cannot know when all these prophetic events will come together, but it is obvious that God the Father is moving us toward the climax of history. He intends to *"bring many sons to glory."* It is our destiny. Jesus told us that the generation that sees Israel's restoration will also see His glorious return.[7] How long is a generation? That answer has varied throughout history. A biblical generation is forty years. However, today generational lifespan have been greatly extended. We don't want to miss the point and miss the Kairos moment in history God has given us. We need to start acting out what we really are—"the kingdom come generation." We can finish this thing. We the church of the coming King can finish the great commission and welcome home our King! We just need to believe it and dedicate ourselves to it. Just suppose it is true—that you may live to see Christ's return. Now Francis Schaeffer's question becomes our big question; *"How should we then live?"* I certainly cannot answer that life impacting question for all men but I can respond to it biblically and personally.

The Earth is shifting beneath our Feet

Have you ever lived through an earthquake watching the ground shake under your feet? I lived in Los Angeles during two really big "shakings." It is an unnerving experience. You feel that there is nothing solid or stable to hold on to. I see that kind of earthquake shaking environment coming upon the world today. Those things we once held onto for security are being taken away. We are on a slippery slope with no hand holds on the way down. The 21st century is a kairos moment when God is shaking us. He is the God of the volcano, allowing the once peaceful mountains to blow their tops! The world's financial structures are shaking and falling, as are the world's economies. Religions that speak of peace are threatening us with global wars. Tribalism—be it national, political, or religious, will bring down the mountain of human conflict upon our heads. Even our very families are being blown apart before our very eyes. Who can we turn to in such unstable times?

The True and the False

We must turn to someone or something that has a steady grip on things. One of the "signs of the times" about which Christ warned us is that when the shaking comes there will be the load voices of false prophets saying "peace peace," when there is no peace. Tragically millions, who cannot find their way through the dust clouds and the ash, will turn to man rather than God for their rescue. This ever encroaching growth of government on a world wide scale is a vivid indicator that we are lost in the dust of our own making. Man and his schemes will not save us, yet the Antichrist will campaign on the theme that he alone can bring us peace. He and his one world government will claim to have the solution to all our problems. When he comes with his messiah-like persona, millions will follow him like a Pied Piper.

We, as Christ followers, are to be wise as serpents and harmless as doves. Living in the terminus era should not terrorize us as it does others. We were destined for this. It is our privilege and our calling. We should know how to live during these coming days of shaking and breaking. When the darkness comes—we are to be children of light. When the shaking comes to your house, you have a hand to hold on to. The Lord is our Rock and our strong tower. He will not leave us nor forsake us. Destiny's children, the true church, must use this terrible shaking as an awakening to call us back to our eternal values, perspective, and priorities. So, how should we then live?

A Blessed Hope

When referring to the coming of Christ, Paul tells Titus it is the believer's "blessed hope." [8] He also tells him how we should live in light of His coming. We should live:

> **Denying ungodliness and worldly desires**
> **Live sensibly and righteously**
> **Live godly in this present age**

What Paul is saying is we should get serious about fulfilling Destiny. God has purposes for the terminal generation of which He wants us to be apart. We are to live "sensibly" in this present age. I take that as an admonition to let go your tight-fisted grip on your "stuff." Let God's shaking loosen your grip on the accumulation of things that are not eternal. You and I need to discern the vast difference between what we need and what we selfishly want or to which we feel entitled. For multitudes of those living in the Eschaton (the God ordained climax of history) there is a need to be shaken loose from those things that bind us and hold us to this world system.

We need not only to be shaken loose, but we need to re-prioritize. Living as though Christ is coming in your lifetime will vastly reshape your priorities. It will answer questions like; *"what* am I living for? or "what am I here for?" We can take Jesus seriously when He urges us to "seek first the Kingdom of God." It will bring into your focus how urgent it is that we invest our time, talent, energies and finances in fulfilling the great commission. We as Christ's people have been sadly neglectful in doing this. Statistics tell us that .97 cents of every church dollar stays in the United States, and is used to tell only 3% of the world's population about Christ. This means we are preaching to the choir! The 97% of the world that really needs to hear the gospel receives less than 3% of the funding to do so.

Fulfilling the Great Commission in our lifetime

In spite of our self-centered focus, God is turning hearts to himself. There is a growing movement of God's Spirit to tell the billions of unreached people about Christ. There is a shaking in the church for missions –that is not yet an earth quaking, but it is a shaking. In January of 2009, Stephen Douglass, president of Campus Crusade for Christ, spoke at the Call2All Congress in Dayton Ohio. He was very positive about how he sees God moving mightily to fulfill the Great Commission. In his speech he said:

"It's not going to be 'business as usual' for the church anymore, we are experiencing increasing shakings all around the world; this is a prelude to the greatest ingathering into God's Kingdom we have ever seen. The time is now! It is imperative we plan and work together to see the Great Commission completed." Douglass further believes we can fulfill this commission from Christ in the next decade. In spite of so much indifference we see in the church, God is answering prayers for the nations. He is quickening hearts to receive Christ in the most difficult and unreached areas.

India

Just look at the shaking going on in India. Although India is a "closed" nation to Christian missions, the body of Christ is growing by leaps and bounds in this country. In 2002, only 2% of India's population was reported as baptized Christian. Then in 2005 the percentage increased to 7%. Today in 2010 it is estimated that 10-

12% of India's population are Christian. It may be even higher because persecution has forced much of the church underground. There are probably 100 million Christ followers in India today.

China

China is another miracle story of God's shaking a nation. When the communists took over China in 1949 there were only 2 million Christians in mainland China. Today some sixty years later there are over 130 million! All this growth is happening in a closed culture and under adverse circumstances. My missionary friends in China tell me that thousands are being saved each month. The red dragon is not so red after all! The terminal generation is shaping destiny for millions.

Africa

In all my years of ministry in Africa, I have never before seen the hunger for Christ as we are seeing today. All over Africa, entire unreached people groups (tribes) are coming to faith in Christ for salvation. Amidst immense problems of poverty, disease and war, millions are being saved. Muslims are finding Christ as Savior along with those coming out of primitive tribal religions. It is a wonder to behold. Those of us doing mission ministry in Africa are all reporting the same story. Africa is aflame for Christ! Africa is no longer just a mission field—it is becoming a mission force. Some of the churches' greatest leaders are coming out of Africa. African missionaries are now going abroad to share Christ in other nations. You might think, "Well it is about time! European missionaries came to Africa in the 1820's." However, this African explosion has taken place AFTER the American and European missionaries left. Africans are winning their own continent to Christ. It is a shaking of God.

Let's finish it

Why is finishing the great Commission so critically important? First, because God loves all mankind He wants to draw the lost into His family of faith. We must tell the nations of His love. My credo for many years has been that no man has the right to hear the Gospel twice until every man has heard it once. Western

DESTINY: YOU AND GOD

civilization has heard the old, old story so many times it has become just that—an old story. Evangelism to the unreached and the least reached are very high on God the Father's list of priorities. It must also be on ours.

Our destiny at this time in "His-Story" is to care about what God cares about—taking the good news to all the nations. Secondly, we can finish this charge Christ has given us. He promises He will come to establish His kingdom and we can hasten His return by being on mission. It is our destiny to accomplish this task. Today just over 60% of the earth's peoples have been reached for Christ. However, this is not a daunting defeat but rather a grand opportunity. With the communications we have at our disposal and the technology we possess today we can lead millions into the family of God. All we need is the vision to see it and the will to accomplish it. It is our destiny to bring us to our destination.

DESTINY POINTERS:

1. Christ has called us to "watch and pray, for you know not what hour your Lord will come." What would you have to change in your daily life to become more watchful?
2. Priorities, values, focus, and purpose are all vital to living in the terminal generation. How are you doing in these areas? Are you living for eternity or for the "here and now"? What areas can you change or re-prioritize?
3. In Matthew 24:14 Jesus tells us He will not return until all the nations hear the Gospel message of salvation. My fellow seminary students and I were convinced that this was unfolding before our very eyes because of radio, then television. Is it now the internet? I don't know but have you mined the depths of your thoughts as to how this might play out? Study scripture, ask for God's insight and see what you can come up with. It is exciting to think about!
4. How can we who have children and grandchildren prepare them for the coming Storm? Think specifically, pray specifically and follow through specifically.

Chapter Twenty

Finding Significance through Destiny Fulfilled

Moving from survival to success, to significance thru an envisioned destiny.

When you are young you do not think much about significance. Somewhere early on it really needs to occur to us that we must live a significant life or we will miss our God—given destiny. Sadly, youth do not think much about living a significant life that makes a difference to God and man. Regrettably, it is the older generation who worries about a wasted life and fear that their life message was not significant.

Yearbook

In a nostalgic moment I was looking thru my old (as in antique) high school yearbook. In the front pages there was an interview with graduating seniors asking what and where you want to be 25 years from now. Reading through the answers, I was struck by how shallow they all were. Most wanted to be rich or famous and live a successful, affluent life. They wanted to live the American dream; which basically is about the accumulation of stuff.

Success and the American Dream

Coming out of high school we were all young and naïve. Life has to teach us the hard way that pursuing the American dream can turn into a nightmare. So often the pursuit of success leads us away from fulfillment and destiny. By nature, success and significance are incompatible. By that I do not mean that men and women of destiny are not successful—many times they are. However they did not fulfill their God appointed destiny by seeking success. Success for them came as by product, it was not a primary goal. People of destiny desire significance not success, and there is a vast difference between the two. Success is about achieving, doing, accumulating and acquiring. Significance is about destiny. It is about making an eternal difference—a legacy that matters to God.

Significance

This quest to fulfill destiny can be confounding. This confusion arises because we can become successful through diligence and hard work. We can pursue success but we cannot pursue significance. Think about it; if you choose to be a significant person you are focused on yourself and you become self centered and prideful. "Look at me, aren't I a significant person!" You see, it doesn't work that way. We cannot seek significance. What we can seek is to fulfill destiny by giving ourselves completely to God and allowing Him to work in and through us to shape us until we are "difference-makers" in this world. Men and women of significance became significant by loving God and serving others.

Success

Every day we meet people who are driven to be successful. Their ambition is to live the American dream. Most Americans interpret that dream as being successful if you possess certain things. Most folks who are driven by the need to succeed, measure their success by three things:

> **Wealth=** they measure a man by what he possesses;
> **Power=** they measure a man by what he controls;
> **Intellect=** they measure a man by what he knows.

DESTINY: YOU AND GOD

Although it is a false assumption, millions chase success as if it were the great good and the grand goal of life. The need to succeed will put you in the performance trap and multitudes are ensnared by it.

A few years ago I heard Cowboy poet J. B. Allen recite some of his great poetry. One of my favorites says:

> *Them 8 to 5's will kill you boys,*
> *There ain't no pride in that.*
> *Each day will forge another link of chain;*
> *Till your spirit like an eagle caged, is walking in its scat.*
> *And no vestige of its majesty remains!*

Even an ole cowboy can see it even if we don't. God never intended that your life be like the Lord of The Rings. We are not put on this earth to chase an elusive "ring" that will fulfill us.

Meet King Solomon

Centuries ago God warned us about this caged living by showing us the life of a great man who had it all but failed to find significance. Solomon, son of David, is the Bible's object lesson in how not to live your life. He sought success and nearly missed significance. His story is told in detail in 1st Kings, but we learn much by reading Solomon's own summations of his quest for success. The book of Ecclesiastes is his autobiographical sketch of a man's history of living for the wrong things. Solomon gave himself to the big three… wealth, power, and knowledge. He was a wise man, a powerful man, and a wealthy man. He was a success in every way that we today measure success. They make TV series about guys like Solomon—*Lifestyles of the Rich and Famous*. Yet at the end of his days he saw the emptiness of a wasted life.

Success and Knowledge

We should have learned from Solomon, but we haven't. Americans are obsessed with education, degrees and knowledge. Science is king in the world today. Somehow we haven't got it figured out that being smart does not make a man good or significant. Thomas Jefferson is quoted as saying "Sin is ignorance". Thus, if we could educate our people we could do away with sin. Man o' man did he ever get that wrong! Teddy Roosevelt knew better. Teddy said that a railroad bum can steal a ride in a railroad car, but if you send him to Harvard and get him a Doctorate, the bum will steal the whole railroad! All education does is make us more clever devils. Greed educated only increases the grasp. Today the biggest crooks are those smart guys at Enron, the knights of Wall Street and politicians.

Knowledge flunked out God

When you and I seek knowledge without the knowledge of God and His purposes, we, like Solomon will eventually cry out... *"And I set my mind to know wisdom and to know madness and folly; I realized that this also is striving after wind. Because in much wisdom there is much grief, and increasing knowledge results in increasing pain."* [1] Which leads me to ask a pointed question; "How smart is the man who knows everything except the one thing that really matters??" If a man doesn't know why he was born and why God put him here—he isn't very smart!

Power and Wealth can Intoxicate

Much the same could be said for Solomon and all his power and wealth. He amassed a fortune and ruled an empire. Jews to this day speak of the "glory days of Solomon." Yet Solomon, for all his women, power, and wealth called all that success—"emptiness." Perhaps we need to ask why there is little fulfillment in power, wealth, and knowledge. Solomon found the answer and shares it with us at the end of his soliloquy in Ecclesiastes.

> *"The conclusion, when all has been heard, is: fear God and keep His commandments, because this applies to every person."* [2]

Bring my coffin to the Party

When I was pastoring in Beverly Hills, California I was often invited to speak all over the United States. Being in Beverly Hills I rubbed shoulders with many very wealthy people and had begun

DESTINY: YOU AND GOD

to feel at ease in the presence of wealth and celebrities. I received an invitation to come to Dallas, Texas for a week of preaching at a church. The pastor of that church took me to meet a very wealthy and notorious "sinner." His name was O.L. Nelms. I tell you his name because he is long deceased and was very public about his wicked ways.

O.L. Nelms was a flamboyant, loud millionaire Texan. He made his money in many places—some of which were very questionable. He liked to brag about his wealth and even had billboards all over Dallas County that read, *"Thanks for helping O. L. Nelms make another Million."*

Mr. Nelms personal assistant was a fine Christian lady. When Nelms was older and dying from cancer, she told her pastor that Mr. Nelms needed a preacher because he was dying and facing a godless eternity. Thus, when I arrived in Dallas, an appointment was made with the infamous O.L. Nelms.

Just before our visit together, Mr. Nelms ran an Ad in the Dallas Morning News that set the town a buzzing. He told the people of Dallas that he had rewritten his Will and donated $1,000,000 to perpetuate a continual beer party to be held in his honor. He would buy the booze for all who attended. The only requirement was that they bring him in his coffin to each and every party! You bring the coffin—I'll buy the beer! That was O.L. Nelms.[3]

Who is Rich?

I wish I could tell you that my time with Mr. Nelms in his penthouse apartment was a blessing and benefit to him. It was not. I told him God loved him and Christ died to forgive him if only he would repent and seek God's mercy. The old man was caustic and arrogant to me and the gospel. I do remember telling him that there were two men in this penthouse—one rich and the other poor. The rich man was walking out the door and the poor man staying behind. I am rich because I have a life in Christ that is significant, and O.L. Nelms was a poor man because all he had was money. He died and faced God as a penniless beggar.

183

DESTINY: YOU AND GOD

What are you living for?

In summary, we were not put on this planet to be successful, but we are here to live significant lives that fulfill our destiny. If you need to know if you are seeking after success rather than significance (destiny) then I suggest an easy test you can take:

Look at your Date book – it will tell you what is really important to you. We plan our days based on what is on our radar screen. Are there any "destiny happenings" or destiny opportunities in your date book? Does eternal significance come from the use of your planning?

If you are not careful to plan for it—there will be no room for destiny.

Look at your Checkbook—it will tell you what you value most. If your wealth is spent on just "stuff" and more "stuff", you are not living a life of significance. We must purposefully invest in the Kingdom to achieve Kingdom significance.

Look at your Watch—Where are you investing your time and energy? If you are spending time rather than redeeming the time, you are missing significance. The chronos will tick away and you will miss the kairos moments that make your life significant.

DESTINY POINTERS:

1. Do you see yourself as a favored Son or Daughter, loved by your Father God? Or are you more inclined to be a warrior; subduing kingdoms, fighting battles to win God's favor.
2. Have you learned you cannot pursue significance; but you can choose to live significantly every day?
3. Success is about doing, significance is about being. Are you focused on being a person God can live and love through?
4. What changes would you have to make in your inner attitudes and your daily habits to make significance possible for you?
5. Examine your datebook, checkbook and how you spend your time. Does it reflect who you want to be or who God wants you to be?

CHAPTER TWENTY ONE

Destiny and the Kingdom of God

Heaven just got better than you ever imagined!

We cannot conclude a book about God-given destiny without a good word on our FINAL destiny—after we die. God's final destination for His children is not heaven as we typically think of it. Our destiny is not to sit on a cloud strumming a harp, or floating around heaven with angels for eternity. Our final destination is to reign with Christ in His Kingdom. It took me a few years to really understand this, but Christ followers are not destined to just die and go to heaven so much as we are destined for the Kingdom that is coming. Listen to the prayer Christ taught us to pray:

> "Our Father who art in heaven,
> Hallowed be Thy name
> Thy kingdom come
> Thy will be done,
> on earth as it is in heaven."[1]

Here are three strong indicators that point the way to our final destiny and rewards for serving Christ:

First, Father/God is planning a big family reunion. He even told us to pray for it. We are to pray for the Kingdom of God to come on earth. The God who created mankind and put him in Eden's garden is going to restore the earth to its original glory. Paul says that all of creation is "groaning" in travail until the coming of the Kingdom. Until that is accomplished, our destiny and God's purpose is not complete. Romans 8:21 tells us that all of creation *"will itself be set free from its slavery to corruption into the freedom of the glory of the children of God."* God's Story is about both our redemption and earth's RESTORATION! We know much about the redemption theme in God's Story, but few seem to understand clearly the strong "restoration" theme. It is this restoration narrative in the Bible that reshapes our thinking about heaven.

The second remarkable indicator of our future is that God's Kingdom and His rule is to be on the Earth—not just in heaven! Jesus is telling us to pray for heaven on earth! How about that? God, the Master Architect, is planning a new earth and new heavens.

That brings us to the third indicator of our final destiny. A day is coming when God's perfect will is accomplished "on earth" the exact same way it is in heaven. The wickedness we see every day in this corrupt world of ours is to be replaced by the kingdom of God—on the earth. At least two realities are necessary to have a "kingdom". One, you must have a king, a sovereign ruler. That would be Jesus Christ. Two; you must have inhabitants who serve the king. That would be us—God's destiny children, on a renewed earth, serving our King.

A Review of God's Story

How can this "kingdom come" prayer become a reality? Let's review the destiny story of the Bible to understand the plot more clearly. Genesis tells us God created the earth, its solar system, and its inhabitants. His creation of mankind seems to be His reason for creating it all. God put man in a perfect Garden, and gave him dominion over it all. Eden's garden is paradise on earth. God and man are there together in perfect fellowship.

Major themes in the Story

As the story unfolds, paradise is lost through Adam's rebellion.

DESTINY: YOU AND GOD

Cast out of Eden, all seems lost. But wait, God has a plan. He promises to redeem man and to restore Eden to its original state. Notice there are two themes running together—redemption and restoration. Most of the Old Testament stories are pointing to the bigger story, God's redemption of mankind. Over 300 times the scriptures indicate a Savior is coming. He is the Messiah, the Son of David. The invasion is coming!

The Invasion Story

Just as the serpent invaded Eden to tempt man and destroy God's paradise, even so, the Son of David, God's messiah, comes down from heaven into Satan's world to invade and destroy his dominion. Scripture says Christ came into the world *"to destroy the works of the Devil"*.[2] It is a drama for the ages, the battle is on; God and Satan, good and evil going head to head and toe to toe. Jesus is here to both redeem and to restore. He is the King bringing His Kingdom with Him. When Jesus was questioned about the mission of John the Baptist, Jesus said John was working in the spirit of Elijah "restoring all things".[3] John's prophetic ministry begins the restoration. Christ, like a mighty warrior, will do battle with Satan and defeat him by means of His own death, burial and resurrection. Christ's resurrection is seen by the Apostles as a military conquest. Paul says Christ conquered death, "when he ascended on high, He led captives in His train."[4]

The Conquest

When describing His ministry, Jesus said very little about heaven, but He said much about the Kingdom of God. Matthew's gospel uses the phrase *"kingdom of heaven"* where the other gospels use the term kingdom of God. They are used synonymously. [5] We need to realize heaven is more about a kingdom than it is about a place. Any discussion about heaven must include an understanding of the Kingdom of God. Heaven was never meant to be seen as a place in the "clouds" where good people go when they die. Rather heaven is about the rule and reign of God in the hearts of men. So, follow the story—the Kingdom of God was in

187

the Garden of Eden. God's rule was there. Especially was it there in the children of God—Adam and Eve. When that rule and reign was lost, God took the initiative to restore it. He is still redeeming and restoring by calling many sons and daughters to glory. As His children fulfill destiny they are moving toward the final battle and victory. The total conquest over evil has not taken place. It is coming someday in the future when Christ the King returns with the armies of heaven to fight one last battle with Satan and his servants. That army of saints is made up of heaven's volunteers who willingly join the conflict. Who exactly are they? Revelation calls them the "24 elders". They are the saints of God from the old covenant and the new. They are described for us in Hebrews 12 as *"a great cloud of witnesses"*; they are men and women of faith whose destiny it was to serve God during their lives on earth and have now joined Him in heaven. They are those destined for the Throne, gathered in God's presence to praise and worship Him until the final conflict begins.

Heaven is more than we have imagined

Jesus told us a story of a rich man who died and went to hell. He was in hell not because he was rich but because he failed to live for God and destiny. Jesus also told of a poor man named Lazarus who died and went to heaven. Jesus did not actually say Lazarus went to heaven, but that he went to *"Abraham's bosom."* This is a Semitic idiom for the "presence of God." We can think of it this way. Our loved ones, who died in God's grace, as did Lazarus, are with the Lord. They are in a very good place. However, it is not their final destination or reward. All things in heaven and earth are waiting for the conquest, consummation and coronation. They are with the Lord God, our Father in Heaven, but they are waiting for the kingdom to come on earth—just as it is in heaven.

Heaven and the Kingdom

My mother is with the Lord. She prayed to receive Christ as a 45 year old woman. She died when she was eighty. To help us comprehend what has happened to her and what will happen to her, let me use her as an illustration. When my mom invited Christ into her heart, at that moment she was "born from above"[6] and became a citizen of the kingdom of God. God's reign and rule came into her life. The King and His kingdom indwelt her being. This is what Jesus means when he says, "the kingdom of God is within you."[7] God put His Spirit in her and purposed to fulfill her destiny. In that sense, every child of God has a little piece of heaven in his heart. We live our daily lives as kingdom sons and daughters. When a believer dies as my mother did, we go into the presence of God, totally aware that we are with Him and enjoying His fellowship. However, all those descriptions of heaven with its gates of pearl, streets of gold and other extravagances are not descriptions of heaven. They come from John's vision in Revelation 21. John is given a preview (vision) of the New Jerusalem "coming down out of heaven from God." [8] This is not a vision of heaven or of "Abraham's bosom." This New Jerusalem is a symbolic representation of the kingdom of God after the 1,000 year reign of Christ. So, heaven for those who are there now is wonderful and unimaginably glorious—but the best is yet to come. They are with the Father, waiting for heaven to become the kingdom.

The saints in heaven have complete redemption but not their full restoration. The restoration of "all things" awaits Christ's return together with His saints to defeat evil and establish His kingdom. Those saints in heaven will be given resurrection bodies at that time. Our loved ones in heaven do not as of yet have a resurrection body. They are spirits even as God is spirit. At that kairos moment of Christ's coming, the dead in Christ will be raised as fast as the blinking of an eye. Millions of Christ-followers, both alive and dead together with the Old Testament righteous, will be transformed.[9]

Resurrection and the Kingdom

Our final destiny requires that we have resurrection bodies. When Christ returns He brings with Him all those who have been waiting in Abraham's bosom. They are those disembodied spirits who in an instant receive a new body. This resurrection body is bullet proof! It knows no hunger, thirst, sorrow, pain or death. It is an eternal body as durable as Christ himself. They become Christ's army, ready for the battle of the ages.

Armageddon

So let the battle begin! Revelation 19 vividly describes Armageddon as a terrible supernatural conflict. All those who served the Beast (antichrist) will perish. Millions will die in the battle. As bad as it will be, and it will be very bad—this fight is fixed; we are destined to win! We cannot lose because if God is for us—who in this world can stand against us? The armies of God are fighting for the kingdom. Earth must have its rightful Ruler restored. The kingdoms of this world must become the kingdoms of our God and of His Christ. We will fight for our destiny and by God's mighty hand we will win. Satan and his servant antichrist will be cast into the bottomless pit. Then Christ our King and His destiny-followers will establish His kingdom on earth.

Eden Restored

God's Story has a marvelous destiny ending. You could even say the ending is a new beginning. The kingdom of God with the Son of David as its King is to become a restored Eden. Mankind's destiny will be accomplished in and through the 1,000 year reign of Christ. God creates a new heaven and a new earth. That means all things will be as they were before Adam's sin and the fall. The laws of sin and death will be no more. The survival of the fittest, the law of the tooth and fang are cancelled. The lion will lie down with the Lamb. We will live in a restored Kingdom with no death, sorrow, sin, hunger or thirst. Paradise restored!

Bible students cannot agree on how long Christ's millennial kingdom will last. Some affirm it is a literal 1,000 years, then Christ turns His kingdom over to the Father.[10] Others think the "1,000 years" may be symbolic of eternity or a long period of time but with an ending. We must leave that up to God. However long the "Kingdom Come" experience is; it will be long enough for us to fulfill our destiny. Your destiny is not to sit idly for eternity

DESTINY: YOU AND GOD

playing harps with angels. We are destined to rule and reign with Christ over a new paradise.

The Messianic Kingdom

The idea that God's kingdom will have rulers as administrators is an ancient one. One very good reason the Jewish scriptures, called the Torah, do not tell us much about heaven as our final destination is that the Hebrew prophets were focused on the Messiah and his kingdom. They were much more interested in the Messianic kingdom than with any idea of going to heaven. Isaiah, Israel's great prophet, foretold Messiah's reign,

> "For a child will be born to us, a son will be given to us; And the government will rest on His shoulders; and His name will be called Wonderful Counselor, Mighty God, Eternal Father, Prince of Peace. There will be no end to the increase of His government or of peace, on the throne of David and over his kingdom, to establish it and to uphold it with justice and righteousness, From then on and forevermore. The zeal of the Lord will accomplish this."[11]

By the time of Christ (messiah), this wonderful prophecy of a coming savior/redeemer and his kingdom became a distorted tribal fantasy. Rabbis were talking of the messianic kingdom as though the Jews would rule the world and each Jew would have thousands of gentile slaves. A kingdom that was spiritual in nature and destined to bless all mankind was made to be physical, material, tribal and militaristic.

A Mother and her Sons

This explains why Jesus' followers were expecting Him to raise an army and overthrow the Romans. You can see this confusion when the mother of James and John comes to Jesus and asks for favored positions for her sons;[12] she wants them to be secretary of state and secretary of the treasury. That's one aggressive mom! Yet it does show us clearly the Jews of Jesus' day were thinking of the messiah and his kingdom, if albeit in distorted terms.

Jesus promises Kingdom Authority

Jesus did not throw the baby out with the bathwater. He knew their kingdom ideas were material and self serving, but He still continued to affirm the coming of God's Kingdom. He let His followers know that they would have a significant part in its administration. He told the twelve; *"Truly I say to you, that you who have followed me, in the regeneration when the Son of Man will sit on His glorious throne, you also shall sit upon twelve thrones, judging the twelve tribes of Israel."* [13] I do not pretend to know what that means, but I do know this declaration has great potential for all Christ-followers. We are destined to have authority and dominion in Christ's kingdom. We already have it now in spiritual matters. Jesus has given us the keys to the kingdom of heaven.[14] We already have Kingdom Keys to unlock doors in the spirit realms. In the coming Kingdom on earth we will have even greater dominion, rule and authority. We will be kings and priests with Christ as our Lord:

"And have made us kings and priests to our God; and we shall reign on the earth." Revelation 5:10

"If we endure, we shall also reign with Him." 2nd Timothy 2:12

Do you not know that the saints shall rule the world? Do you not know that we shall judge angels? 1st Corinthians 6:2, 3

"And I saw thrones, and they sat on them, and judgment was committed to them. Then I saw the souls of those who had been beheaded for their witness to Jesus and for the word of God, who had not worshiped the beast or his image, and had not received his mark on their foreheads or on their hands. And they lived and reigned with Christ for a thousand years." Revelation 20:4

"There shall be no night there: They need no lamp nor light of the sun, for the Lord God gives them light. And they shall reign forever and ever." Revelation 22:5

DESTINY: YOU AND GOD

"His lord said to him, 'Well done, good and faithful servant; you were faithful over a few things, I will make you ruler over many things. Enter into the joy of your lord." Matthew 25:21

This is your Final Destination

Are you getting this? I pray so! You do not have to die to go to heaven because we as Christ-followers have the kingdom of heaven within us. We are to reign in life even as we are destined to reign in the next life. By fulfilling your kingdom destiny here and now, you shall be rewarded as a good and faithful servant by ruling and reigning with Christ in the kingdom of God. Heaven certainly looks more appealing than it used to! You and I should be determined to live out our destiny calling, for great is our reward in the kingdom of heaven. Surely our greatest reward will be to hear our Savior say to us, "well done, my child, well done!"

This leads me to say, that reigning and ruling in the coming kingdom will not be the joy that rings your bell. Remember Jesus told James and John that the greatest in the kingdom would be the one who served others the most. He said the first would be last and the last would be first. Our greatest pleasure in heaven will be the manifested presence of God. In John's vision in Revelation 21 he sees the tabernacle of God in the midst of the kingdom saints. God has "pitched His tent among them." Later in the vision John sees there is no temple of God in the holy city Jerusalem, because God Himself is the temple and His presence is the light of the city. There is no need for electricity, sun, moon or stars. God is the light of the kingdom. He is everywhere—manifested. That will be our greatest reward for fulfilling destiny. Your final destination is to be with the Father. You and God will be as one in total unity and fellowship—that is heaven and joy unspeakable!

After the 1,000 years

What comes after the kingdom reign of Christ on earth with His saints? No one can say for certain. How long will it take us to finish our dominion, accomplish our tasks, and glorify our Savior I do not know, but at some point the Kingdom of Christ will be turned over to God the Father. Paul tells us, *"then comes the end, when He delivers up the kingdom to the God and Father, when He has abolished all rule and all authority and power. For He must reign until He has put all His enemies under His feet."*[15] Scripture, especially in Revelation, is very symbolic and mystical about our final destiny after the millennium. We can take great comfort in the fact that an eternity is coming without Satan, sin, or temptation. Maybe there are other worlds to conquer, as the favored Sons of God go streaking through the universe proclaiming God's glory to all who will listen. I cannot wait!

DESTINY POINTERS

1. Take time to read the story of Lazarus in Luke 16:19-31. Notice Lazarus in Abraham's bosom and the rich man in hell both have all of their senses: sight, smell, taste and touch. How does this change your perception of heaven? Note: This is the only parable Christ told which uses personal names. Does this make it more factual than narrative?
2. What do you think the kingdom will look like on a new earth and new heavens? Since there is no sin, selfishness, conflict, tears or death—what will a day be like for you?
3. Think of those believers you knew who have died. Knowing that your future includes being with them, how does that impact you?
4. Does the future conflict excite or frighten you? Are you going to be on the winning side? How can you have certainty that your eternal future is secure?
5. Are you currently being "faithful over a few things"? If you are not, are you willing to change your priorities in life to become so?
6. If you were to courageously live for "kingdom come" destiny, what relationships, values and priorities would have to be altered –forever? Would others who know you recognize you as a kingdom citizen?
7. What does the idea of "laying up treasures in heaven" mean to you? How do you invest in heaven's bank?

Chapter Twenty Two

But I was Afraid . . .

Investing your life in the things that really matter.

Jesus told many stories to illustrate the Kingdom of God; one of His most disturbing is called the "Parable of the Talents." It is a story about investment – in destiny.

"It's also like a man going off on an extended trip. He called his servants together and delegated responsibilities. To one he gave five thousand dollars, to another two thousand, to a third one thousand, depending on their abilities. Then he left. Right off, the first servant went to work and doubled his master's investment. The second did the same. But the man with the single thousand dug a hole and carefully buried his master's money.

"After a long absence, the master of those three servants came back and settled up with them. The one given five thousand dollars showed him how he had doubled his investment. His master commended him: 'Good work! You did your job well. From now on be my partner.' "The servant with the two thousand showed how he also had doubled his master's investment. His master commended him: 'Good work! You did your job well. From now on be my partner.'

"The servant given one thousand said, 'Master, I know you have high standards and hate careless ways, that you demand the best and make *no allowances for error. I was afraid I might disappoint you, so I found a good hiding place and secured your money. Here it is, safe and sound down to the last cent.*

"*The master was furious. 'That's a terrible way to live! It's criminal to live cautiously like that! If you knew I was after the best, why did you do less than the least? The least you could have done would have been to invest the sum with the bankers, where at least I would have gotten a little interest.*

"*Take the thousand and give it to the one who risked the most. And get rid of this "play-it-safe" who won't go out on a limb. Throw him out into utter darkness.'* Matthew 25:14-30, The Message

The master's reaction to the servant who was paralyzed by fear is very revealing. It tells us how God feels about a wasted life and failed destiny. The Master in the story is God, and He calls this one talent servant a *"play it safe'* kind of guy *"who won't go out on a limb."* Ouch! Notice the servant wasn't a thief—he didn't steal the money, but rather he buried it. He still had the investment money, but because of fear, he failed to invest it. In so doing, he failed his master and his calling. He was a poor steward of the master's trust in him.

I was Afraid

Did you notice the image the one talent servant had of his master? He sees him as having unattainable standards, being totally impatient with any mess ups, and always demanding the best. Most revealing is his perception of his master as *"making no allowances for error."* Sadly this is how millions of religious people perceive God to be. They have little concept of God as their Father, or any idea that we can be partners in the family business. They are so fearful of disappointing God that they fail to do anything significant or destiny fulfilling. What are you afraid of that is keeping you from going all out for Christ? I know you can see the Kingdom and destiny right in front of you, but you won't risk it or refuse to believe it is there for you. Why? Is it because you cannot believe God really wants you in His story? Well, He does—so go for it! Don't play it safe, he will reward your risk. He is waiting for you to invest your talents in things eternal. Under no circumstances do you want Him to return and find you patting the dirt down on your buried life.

Wickedness Redefined

Jesus tells us God does not honor, pamper or protect our fears. He says to the fear-filled servant, *"that's a terrible way to live! It's criminal to live cautiously like that! If you knew I was after the best, why did you do less than the least?"* The master then calls him a "wicked servant." Now that's different. We usually think of wickedness in terms of evil behaviors far exceeding that of hiding money for fear of loss. Yet, in God's economy "playing it safe" and fearing to reach for destiny is a terrible way to live—it is even criminal! The Father expects you to fulfill His purposes that are "from the womb." You were brought into this world for the very purpose of fulfilling Destiny. He expects His children to excel, to soar like eagles, to conquer kingdoms for His Names Sake. I want to challenge you to look carefully at your life, its values and the impact you are making. What do you see? Better yet, what has God shown you? If you are not a destiny player, then go dig up your buried talent and dedicate the remainder of your days to investing in Eternity. If you'll do that—your destiny awaits you and your King's smile will be upon you.

DESTINY POINTERS:

1. What is your greatest fear? Is it the fear of failure? I challenge you to ask God to reveal Himself to you and His Destiny purposes for your remaining days. Then ask Him to encourage your heart with enough faith to cast out the fear!
2. Can you sit down and take a careful look at where in your life have you continually "played it safe"? Some of those areas belong to God and your Destiny. Is it time to go for broke and risk to reach?
3. What has God blessed you with and what can you do to use it to bless Him? List what is most important to you. Compare this to the list God might make that is important to Him.
4. In the parable of the talent there is marked difference between

"faithful" and "unfaithful" service to God. Examine your own life to see where you might be unfaithful with your talents. How can you become faithful with your talents?

5. If you are retired have you buried your talent? Sometimes the best eternal service can be achieved after you are "retired" because you are free – financially and time wise –to pursue God's destiny, but don't wait until then!

Epilogue

Every author concludes a book with mixed emotions. One is relief—the task is done. Another emotion is doubt—will anyone be blessed by what's been written. Deep in my spirit is a hope that you and thousands of others will begin to walk on destiny's pathway. So many in this crazy world are lost to all that is meaningful, or significant; they live without hope. It need not be that for you. Your destiny journey begins in a decision to make Christ Jesus your Lord and Savior. Then to those who are already Christ-followers, it is my prayer that you are quick to believe you can and should be a player in God's redemptive Drama. Live out your destiny till the King and His Kingdom come.

> "To every man there openeth
> A way & ways and a way:
> The high soul treads the high way,
> And the low soul gropes the low,
> And in between on the misty flats,
> The rest drift to & fro."
> John Oxenham

My prayer for you is that you not live the rest of your days, "drifting to and fro" but that God's potential is fulfilled in your life.

The Message translates Paul's prayer for the Ephesians like this:

> "I ask the God of our Master, Jesus Christ, the God of glory—to make you intelligent and discerning in knowing him personally, your eyes focused and clear, so that you can see exactly what it is He is calling you to do, grasp the immensity of this glorious way of life He has for His followers, oh, the utter extravagance of His work in us who trust him—endless energy, boundless strength! Ephesians 1:18

Friend, we are Destined for the throne—see you there!

—Barry Wood
Dallas, Texas

FOOTNOTES

Verses that do not include translation reference have been paraphrased by author.

Foreword
1. Greenslade, Philip, *A Passion for God's Story: Discovering your place in God's strategic plan.* Paternoster, 2006. Print. p24

Chapter One - From your Mother's Womb
1. Clifford, Clark M., and Richard C. Holbrooke. *Counsel to the President: a Memoir.* New York: Random House, 1991. Print. p22
2. McCullough, David G. *Truman.* New York: Simon & Schuster, 1992. Print. p620
3. Esther 4:14 NIV
4. Galatians 1:15, 16 KJV

Chapter Two - Fated is not Destined
1. Proverbs 16:9 (NIV)
2. Goldsworthy, Graeme. *According to Plan: the Unfolding Revelation of God in the Bible.* Downers Grove, IL: InterVarsity, 2002. Print. Chapter 3.

   Author's note: This fine work is a classic in presenting the Bible as narrative, God's Big Story.

Chapter Three - The Bible: God's Destiny Story
1. Genesis 1:24 & 2:8, 15

Chapter Four - Covenant Men are Men of Destiny
1. Greenslade, Philip, *A Passion for God's Story: Discovering your place in God's strategic plan.* Paternoster, 2006. Print. pp52-64 contain a full description of the impact of God's covenant with Noah.
2. Wright, Christopher. *Deuteronomy.* Peabody, MA: Hendrickson, 1996. Print. *p57*
3. Matthew 23:37, 38 (NAS)
4. Great Britain partitioned lands for the Jews to return after World War II. The Belfour Declaration was seen by Bible students as fulfillment of ancient promises of a restored Israel in Ezekiel, Isaiah and Jeremiah.
5. Jeremiah 31:31ff predicts the coming of Messiah to establish a new covenant of grace; then Hebrews 8:13 and 9:15 tell us the old covenant is obsolete and Christ is the mediator of a new covenant.

Chapter Five – Destiny and Religion
1. Ephesians 2:8, 9 (NAS)

DESTINY: YOU AND GOD

Chapter Six-David's Son – Destined for the Throne
1. 1 John 5:39 NIV
2. Luke 24:25-27 NASV
3. Luke 2:21 In Hebrew, "Joshua" from the verb yashav meaning "to save". The Greek equivalent of Joshua is Jesus
4. Luke 2: 25-35
5. Romans 5:8 (NAS)
6. Hebrews 2:10 (NAS)
7. Romans 8:29 (NAS)
8. Isaiah 53:4-6 (NIV)
9. John 11:25 (NIV)
10. John 14:19 (NAS)
11. 1 Corinthians 15:6
12. Matthew 6:10 (NAS)

Chapter Seven - Destiny and Your Salvation
1. John 3:16 (NAS)
2. Romans 5:8 (NAS)
3. Revelation 13:8 (author's paraphrase)
4. Acts 4:12 (NAS)
5. Romans 8:30 (NAS)
6. John 3:36 (NAS)
7. Romans 5:14, 18
8. Ephesians 2:10 (NAS)

Chapter Eight - Your Personal Destiny and the "Kairos"
1. For an account of Dixie Howell's achievements see: travel/yos/legends/football/dixie-howell.cfm
2. Strobel, Lee. *The Case for Christ*. Zondervan Pub. House, 1998. Print. Narrative about Louis Lapides as a leader among the Hebrew-Christian community.

Chapter Nine - Seizing those Destiny Moments as Opportunities
1. Galatians 6:10 (NAS)
2. Acts 16:10 (NAS)
3. Mark 4:35-41
4. Evangecube. Patent.

Evangecube is a gospel witnessing tool that functions like a Rubik's Cube. It has pictures on each panel that tell the story of Christ. Most Evangecubes are small but this large E-cube is used with larger groups.

5. Colossians 1:27 (NAS)

Chapter Ten - Destiny and Pre-Destiny
1. Babcock, Maltbie. *This Is My Father's World*. 1901. CD.
2. Romans 8:28 (NAS)
3. Ephesians 1:4-5 and 3:11 (NIV)
4. Romans 8:29 (NIV)
5. 1 Corinthians 2:7 (NIV)
6. Romans 8:30-31 (NIV)
7. Jeremiah 29:11 & 13
8. 1 Timothy 2:3-4 (NIV)
9. Lamentations 3:23 (KJV)
10. Romans 8:31 (NIV)

Chapter Eleven - What a difference a Day Makes
1. Mark 15:21 (NAS)
2. Acts 2:5-10 (NAS)
3. Acts 6:5 and Acts 13:1

Chapter Twelve - Men of Vision Fulfill Destiny
1. Proverbs 29:18 (KJV)
2. Acts 26:19 (NAS)
3. Proverbs 16:9
4. Matthew 6:33 (NAS)
5. 2 Samuel 23:20
6. Chambers, Oswald. *My Utmost for His Highest*. Uhrichsville, OH: Barbour Pub., 2007. Print.
7. 1 Kings 19:4
8. 2 Corinthians 1:8, 9 (NAS)
9. Philippians 3:14 (NAS)

Chapter Thirteen - Your Destiny can be Your Legacy
1. James, William. *Famous Quotes and Quotations at BrainyQuote*. Web.
2. Chapman, J. Wilbur. *Believersweb*. Web.

Chapter Fourteen - Who You Are and Who You Really Are
1. 1 Corinthians 16:13, 14 (NAS)
2. Galatians 5:22, 23
3. Psalms 22:10; Psalms 139:13; Galatians 1:15
4. Psalms 37: 4, 5 (NAS)
5. 2 Timothy 1:6
6. 1 Corinthians 1: 26-29 NLT

7. Exodus 4: 10-12

Chapter Fifteen - Destiny Demands Defiance
1. Genesis 50:20
2. Matthew 16:21
3. Matthew 11:12 (NAS)
4. Bailey, Don. *Just Say YES*. Web.
5. Chambers, Oswald. *My Utmost for His Highest*. Uhrichsville, OH: Barbour Pub., 2007. Print. Author's note: This is my favorite read to inspire me to greatness.
6. Hebrews 5:8
7. Burke, Edmund. *Famous Quotes and Quotations at BrainyQuote*. Web.
8. "William Wilberforce Biography | Biography Online." *Biography Online | Biographies of Inspirational and Famous People*. Web.
9. 2 Samuel 23:20 (NAS)

Chapter Sixteen - The Risk of reaching for Destiny

Chapter Seventeen - Destiny and the Call of God
1. Batterson, Mark. *In a Pit with a Lion on a Snowy Day*. Sisters, Or.: Multnomah, 2006. Print.
2. John Witherspoon was the only minister to sign the 1776 Declaration of Independence. A noted statesman and theologian, he was not a friend of the "enlightenment" movement that swept over New England, espousing rather the moral reasoning of European thinkers.
3. "Aaron Burr" *Appleton's Cyclopedia of American Biography, Edited by James Grant Wilson, John Fiske and Stanley L. Klos. Six Volumes, New York: D. Appleton and Company, 1887-1889 and StanKlos.com 1999*. Web.
4. Romans 8:31-39
5. 1 John 1:9 (NAS)

Chapter Eighteen - Your Destiny as God's Mosaic
1. Genesis 32:22-32
2. Shelly Johnson. *Mosaic of Grace*. David Schober, 2009. CD.

Chapter Nineteen - Destiny and the Terminal Generation
1. When the returning European Jews were given a national homeland in the Belfour Declaration of 1948, Palestine & Jerusalem were partitioned off with areas given to Jews and Palestinians. The Palestinians got that section of "old" Jerusalem that had the Mosque of Omar and the ancient site of Solomon's temple. Therefore, the Jews were not technically nor biblically "home."
2. Daniel 9 and 11, makes reference to a period of "seventy weeks." These are seventy prophetic weeks of years. The 70th week is the seven year

period of "great tribulation" hosted by the abomination of desolation which Jesus alludes to in Matthew 24:15 & 29.
3. Revelation 14:12-13
4. Gundry, Robert Horton. *The Church and the Tribulation*. Grand Rapids, MI: Zondervan, 1973. Print.

   Author's Note: Although not as popular as a pre-tribulation Rapture teaching; there are capable scholars who feel a mid-tribulation Rapture is the true Biblical teaching.
5. Revelations 14:12-13 (NAS)
6. Revelation 12:11 (NAS)
7. Matthew 24: 14
8. Ezekiel 13:10
9. Titus 2:12, 13
10. Matthew 28:19, 20

Chapter Twenty - Finding Significance through Destiny
1. Ecclesiastes 1:17-18 (NAS)
2. Ecclesiastes 12:13 (NAS)
3. "Memorials: Partying Is Such Sweet Sorrow - TIME." *Breaking News, Analysis, Politics, Blogs, News Photos, Video, Tech Reviews - TIME.com*. Web.

Chapter Twenty - One Destiny and the Kingdom of God
1. Matthew 6:10 (NAS)
2. Romans 8:18, 21
3. Revelation 21:1, 2
4. 1 John 3:8 (NAS)
5. Matthew 17:11
6. Ephesians 4:8 (NIV)
7. Matthew 21:43
8. John 3:3
9. Luke 17:21 (KJV)
10. Revelation 21:2 (NAS)
11. 1 Corinthians 15:20-23
12. 1 Corinthians 15:24
13. Isaiah 9:6, 7 (NAS)
14. Matthew 20:20
15. Matthew 19:28 (NAS)
16. Matthew 16:19
17. 1Corinthians 15:24, 25 (NAS)

Chapter Twenty Two - But I was Afraid . . .
Epilogue

BARRY WOOD MINISTRIES

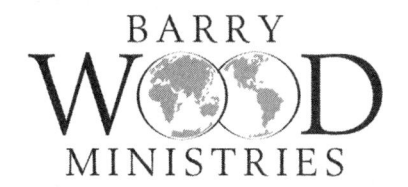

Barry Wood Ministries is reaching tens of thousands with the Gospel in East Africa every month. In 2010 alone the African staff of BWM reached over 2,500,000 people through Aids education in churches and schools; and by using evangelistic films in remote villages.

Since it's inception in 2001, the BWM staff has trained over 100,000 african christians to witness using the Evangecube, and planted churches throughout East Africa. They have also trained 6,000 church leaders to become culture changing agents in their spheres of influence by means of our key man leadship conferences.

Building churches, drilling water wells, training leaders, and intervening in times of crisis, BWM is making an impact in the remote bush of East Africa. We are supported soley by the generousity of ministry partners and friends who too want to make a difference. We invite you to contact us by phone, e-mail, or the Internet.

There are videos and much detailed information about the far reaching influence of BWM on our Web Site. For further information about *"Destiny: You and God"* go to www.barrywoodministries.org; or write us at barry@barrywoodministries.org

Copies of *Destiny: You and God* can be purchased in volumes at discount by ordering thru the BWM offices in Dallas, Texas. Also E-book editions are available @ Amazon.com

BARRY WOOD MINISTRIES

Who we are: Barry Wood Ministries is a missionary Disciple-making organization. We have been active in missions for over 30 years; primarily in East Africa. BWM is focused on leadership training in developing countries. Our goal is to raise up indigenous leaders who can permanently change their culture for Christ.

BWM has four African regional directors who manage & set Vision for their countries.

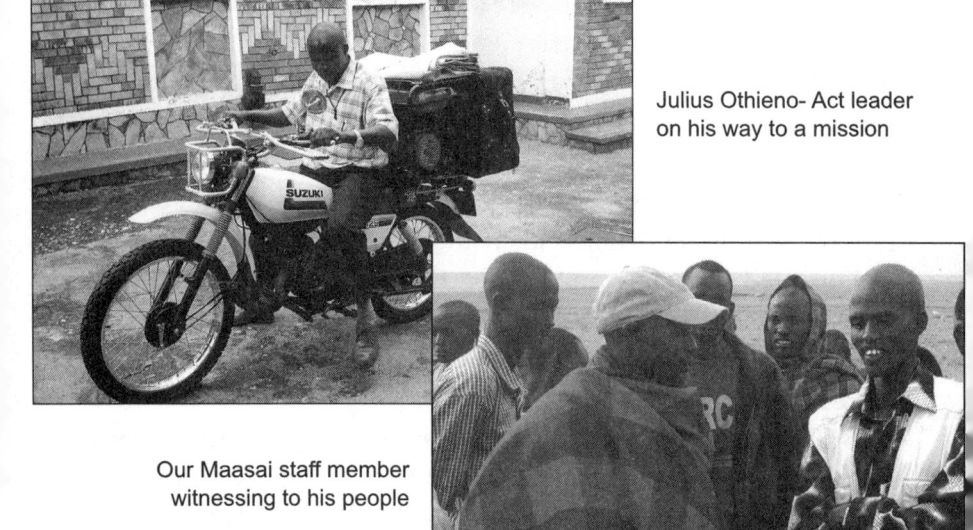

Julius Othieno- Act leader on his way to a mission

Our Maasai staff member witnessing to his people

What we do:
- BWM develops 3rd world Christians into national Leaders.
- BWM educates youth & churches in HIV-Aids awareness.
- BWM evangelizes thru Film ministries & Evangecube training.
- BWM plants churches thru discipleship/evangelism.
- BWM leads mission projects-medical & clean water, orphans & poverty relief.
- BWM equips indigenous missionaries to win their people to Christ & plant Churches.
- BWM develops women as leaders in East Africa.

BWM Leadership Training Graduates

Where we minister: BWM has offices and staff in Uganda, Rwanda, Congo, Tanzania, Kenya and Burundi. Our staff make missionary leaders of ordinary people in out of the way places. Most of our trained leaders live in the bush or smaller villages; living, going, & ministering where others seldom go.

How we do ministry: We seek to find the best people and train them to go, win & disciple others. Over 6,000 indigenous missionaries have been equipped since 2001. Our staff have have trained over 100,000 people to witness using the Evangecube; and the number is growing daily. All this is done thru the free-will love gifts of individuals, churches & foundations.

2009 ACT leaders & BWM Staff

Our African Staff: There are 19 full time staff in East Africa. These are African trained Key men & women who are actively training thousands more to fulfill the great Commission. Our 17 Aids Combat Teams {ACT} are serving in six countries. They are all professionals in Aids education & disciple making. They are culture changing agents wherever they minister.